A Crowd of Witnesses

Interviews with Famous New Testament Men and Women

Enzo Crocetti
Mario Giordano

Translated by Lisa Maroni
Illustrations by Sergio Toppi

Pauline
ST. PAUL BOOKS & MEDIA

Nihil Obstat: Rev. Thomas W. Buckley, S.T.D., S.S.L.
Imprimatur: ✠Bernard Cardinal Law
             May 11, 1994

Crocetti, Enzo.
    [Personaggi del Vangelo. English]
    A crowd of Witnesses. Interviews with famous New Testament men and women
/ Enzo Crocetti, Mario Giordano ; translated by Lisa Maroni ; illustrations by Sergio
Toppi.
         p.   cm.
    ISBN 0-8198-1531-4 (pbk.)
    1. Bible. N.T.—Biography—Juvenile literature. [1. Bible. N.T.—Biography.]
I. Giordano, Mario. II. Toppi, Sergio, ill. III. Title.
BS2433.C7613   1994   94-20697
225.9'22—dc20   CIP
                                                                   AC

Original title: *I personaggi del Vangelo.*

Copyright © 1990, Edizioni Paoline, Milan, Italy.

Translated from the Italian by Lisa Maroni.

Adaptations made by the editorial staff, St. Paul Books & Media

English edition copyright © 1994, Daughters of St. Paul

Printed and published in the U.S.A. by St. Paul Books & Media, 50 St. Paul's
Avenue, Boston, MA 02130.

St. Paul Books & Media is the publishing house of the Daughters of St. Paul,
an international congregation of women religious serving the Church with the
communications media.

1 2 3 4 5 6 7 8 9   99 98 97 96 95 94

CONTENTS

INTRODUCTION

In this second volume on the Bible, Mario Giordano and Enzo Crocetti present the world and main characters of the New Testament. In "rereading" the New Testament in a popular format, the authors have once again fully employed their years of experience as editors of *Il Giornalino*, one of the most widely-circulated weekly magazines for the young. The illustrations of Sergio Toppi again offer a fascinating visual counterpoint to the text.

The first part consists of thirty-two chapters, each dedicated to a New Testament personality. The second part—the appendix—brings to the reader's attention the essential information available about the principal figures of the New Testament, making it easy to identify them and situate them in history.

Each of the thirty-two New Testament personalities is seen individually, by means of those lively, imaginary interviews characteristic of these volumes. The interview is a literary genre, capable of "live" communication. It seems especially suited to stimulating the imagination and curiosity of adolescents, who are invited to live the adventures of the characters first-hand, and to identify with their feelings. A whole gallery of persons is seen through their own words: from Mary the Mother of Jesus to Mary Magdalene; from Herod the bloodthirsty king to Barabbas the robber saved by Jesus; from Peter the head of the apostles to Paul the apostle of the Gentiles. In short, all the key figures of the New Testament tell their story, describing their meeting with Jesus, with his humanity and his miracles, his words of love and his revolutionary commandments.

Each person interviewed talks about "his or her" Gospel, or at least that part of the Gospel they lived in person. But, after reading all these testimonies, we find a picture that is rich and varied but substantially unified. With a wealth of information and historical and religious sensitivity, the various testimonies reconstruct the life and teachings of Jesus, revisited through the words of those who were close to him.

Each interview is preceded by a quote from the New Testament that introduces the key figure, and is accompanied by an inset that treats historical and social topics, offering further background for the stories of the biblical figures themselves.

Silvio Riolfo Marengo

Mary, the Mother of Jesus

"The angel Gabriel was sent from God to a city of Galilee named Nazareth, to a virgin who was betrothed to a man of the house of David named Joseph, and the virgin's name was Mary. And when he came into her presence he said, 'Hail, full of grace, the Lord is with you!... And, behold, you will conceive in your womb and will bear a son, and you shall name him Jesus. He'll be great and will be called Son of the Most High.'"
(Luke 1:26-28, 31-32)

I'm so afraid of saying the wrong thing and spoiling everything. How does someone interview the mother of Jesus?
"Without fear and worry. Just ask me whatever you want to know."

How many Marys are there in the Bible?

"In the entire Bible seven other women are mentioned who have the name Miriam, or Mary. In the Old Testament we find the sister of Moses and Aaron. The sister of Lazarus and Martha was also named Mary. Then there is Mary Magdalen, from whom Jesus 'had driven out seven demons,' and Mary, mother of James and Joseph (both of them were close to me when my son suffered on the cross); then there is Mary of Clopas, and Mary mother of John Mark, a very hospitable woman. The list ends with a Christian from Rome who was affectionately greeted by Paul in one of his letters."

What does the name Mary mean?

"Many scholars have researched the root meaning of this name. A German author wrote a book in which he listed sixty different explanations of the name Mary. Some of the meanings are very imaginative, like 'she who lights up the ocean,' or, 'star of the ocean.' Other meanings are: beautiful, loved, sister, elevated one, exalted one, and noble one."

Were you frightened when the angel appeared to you to announce that you were going to give birth to a son?

"No, I wasn't frightened but I was very uneasy, because it wasn't logical. I didn't know of any previous events like this."

What did your fiancé, Joseph, say to you?

"It was his right to reject me publicly. Both of us knew what would happen to me according to the law if he rejected me and asked for me to be punished. We talked about it for a long time. Joseph was a strong, just man, and he loved me very much. I was sure that he would not reject me. At first Joseph wanted to break our engagement, but secretly. But then one day he came to me. He had changed. He seemed to have aged a little, but his glance was serene and decisive. He assured me that he would always stay close to me. And he did, until his death."

According to the edict of Augustus, only Joseph needed to go to Bethlehem for the census. Why did you go with him?

"The two of us were inseparable. We were always together, no matter what. Plus Joseph wouldn't have left me alone in that condition. I could have had the baby at any moment."

Can you tell me about when Jesus was born?

"While we were in Bethlehem, we stayed in a stable. And it was there that my baby was born. Joseph was happy. Then the shepherds arrived, kind and concerned. They brought us milk, a little bit of cheese, and some pieces of bread. Quite a bit later, we were visited by some strange men. They came from far away and said they had been guided by a star. I was confused, but they were too. They spoke a foreign language, but we managed to understand each other."

What was Bethlehem like?

"I had never been there before. There was a lot of confusion during that time. It was also called Ephrathah, meaning 'rich with fruit': the surrounding area was very fertile. There were many figs, olives, and grapes. It was the homeland of David and his family. 700 years earlier the prophet, Micah, had foretold the extraordinary destiny of this place. He said: 'Out of you [Bethlehem] I will bring a ruler for Israel'" (5:2).

Did anyone know your secret, that you were the mother of God?

"Joseph sensed that we were part of a divine plan. But I myself didn't understand the full meaning of this plan. When we brought Jesus to Jerusalem to offer him to the Lord, we met two old people, a woman and a man. Their names were Simeon and Anna. They both acted as though they knew my secret. They talked as if my son were a long awaited prince come to save the Jewish people. And from that moment, I began to fear for him."

Many painters have depicted you in various poses, and in very different situations. If you were to flip through an album of all of these paintings, which one would you stop to look at?

"Maybe the painting that shows me riding a donkey while holding my baby in my arms. It reminds me of our escape into Egypt. Joseph went ahead of us and never got tired of walking on the sand of the desert. He continued to urge that poor donkey on. He was afraid that Herod would catch us. Joseph made me very anxious, and I couldn't wait to get to Egypt, where we would be safe. I was often plagued by anxiety. I worried about Jesus right up to the day that I saw him on the cross."

Do you remember anything about your stay in Egypt?

"I remember the generosity of our Hebrew people, who had left years before. They had formed a large community and gave us everything we needed. My husband Joseph was a very good carpenter, and he didn't have any trouble finding work. I remember the first steps that Jesus made in that foreign country. I remember when the terrible news arrived about the slaughter ordered by Herod. I remember how kind and hospitable the Egyptians were. They adored cats and crocodiles with a worship that seemed to me more grotesque than idolatrous...."

When the danger had passed, you returned home and settled in Nazareth of Galilee. How did Jesus grow up?

"For the first few years he was always at my side. He held my hand when I went to get water from the well. He watched me while I crushed the grain and made bread. I told him everything that I knew: how the world was created, the sin of our first parents, the flood.... All the things my mother had taught me and that I had heard the rabbis say in the synagogue. Once in a while Jesus would run in to see Joseph in his workshop. Like all mothers, I didn't want him to ever grow up. After a while I began to realize that he was spending more and more time with Joseph. Jesus was growing up and he was beginning to learn the carpenter's trade."

Did you ever scold your son?
"I did so once, in Jerusalem when Jesus was twelve years old. At a certain point we lost him. After desperately looking for him everywhere, we found him in the temple speaking with the teachers of the law. I scolded him for making us worry, and he looked at me and said: 'Didn't you know that I have to concern myself with my Father's affairs?' At the time I didn't really understand what he meant. But that was when I realized that my mission was not to understand, but to remember. In fact I realized this even from the beginning, because I knew that I had given life to the divine Word."

JESUS' DATE OF BIRTH

For centuries Christmas has been celebrated on the twenty-fifth of December. But was Jesus really born on that day? According to some he was, but it is actually more likely that the twenty-fifth of December was chosen because many pagan festivals were held around that date. In Egypt they celebrated the god Horus, symbol of the rising sun; in Rome they celebrated the Saturnalia and the "rebirth" of the sun, which began to lengthen the hours of daylight. Instead of the natural sun, the Christians preferred to celebrate the "spiritual sun," that is Jesus, whose coming brought light to mankind.

And now, the problem of the year of Jesus' birth. We count our years from his birth. That's why our era is called the Christian Era. But are we sure that Jesus Christ was born at the beginning of the first year of this era? The Gospel simply says that he was born in "Bethlehem of Judea at the time of King Herod." This is surely an historical reference , but it does not allow us to establish an exact year. From other sources we know that Herod died in the year 4 B.C., and so the birth was most probably in the sixth year before the Christian Era, or at least sometime between 7 and 4 B.C. The calendar that we still follow was based on an incorrect date. The error was committed by "Dionysius," a monk of the sixth century, who did not have access to the extensive historical information available to us today.

What strikes me in reading the Gospel is your silence. Why have so few of your words been recorded?
"Because my son was the Word. And also you have to remember that women really weren't supposed to speak back then. History was 'written' by men."

After the death of Jesus, what did you do?
"I spent the rest of my life remembering."

Joseph, Mary's Husband

"Now the birth of Jesus came about like this. When his mother Mary was betrothed to Joseph, but before they came together, she was found to be with child by the Holy Spirit. Joseph her husband was a good and upright man so he was planning to put her away, but quietly, because he didn't wish to disgrace her. But while he was thinking these things over, behold, the angel of the Lord appeared to him in a dream and said, 'Joseph, son of David, don't be afraid to take your wife Mary into your house—the child who has been conceived in her is from the Holy Spirit. She'll give birth to a son and you shall name him Jesus, because he'll save his people from their sins.'"
(Matthew 1:18-21)

Who are the ancestors of Jesus?

"I'll tell you about the most famous ones: the patriarch Abraham, his son Isaac, and Jacob, who emigrated to Egypt with his whole family. As my legal son, Jesus was descended from Jacob's son, Judah, and from David, the most famous king of Israel. But the list of Jesus' ancestors is very long."

Could you tell me about some of Jesus' women ancestors?

"Three of the most famous were Tamar, who with Judah had Perez and Zerah; Rahab, the mother of Boaz; and Ruth, who was from Moab. Ruth is known for her goodness and generosity."

What was Galilee like in your time?

"It was a Roman province, located west of the Sea of Galilee. The hillsides were covered with palm trees, olive groves, fig trees, and grape vines. In the small cities and villages many trades were carried on. For example, people exported salted fish, built boats, dyed cloth and made pottery."

Why do most painters paint you as a bearded old man holding a club covered with flowers?

"Because of a legend that said that I was old and widowed, already the father of many children before I married Mary. According to that legend, when Mary turned twelve years old, the priests of the temple decided to have a kind of contest so as to decide whom she should marry. They called all the old, widowed men to lay down their clubs next to the altar of the temple. I was selected because flowers began to grow out of my club. In another version of the legend, a dove flew out of my club. But these are all legends, like the one that says that I died at the age of 111."

What did you do when Mary told you she was expecting a child?

"I was very confused and upset. When these things happen, the woman is supposed to be denounced. But right away I

decided that I couldn't do that, because I loved Mary too much. So I decided instead to break our engagement in secret, without making a fuss."

What made you change your mind?

"In my worst moment of suffering, an angel came to me in a dream. He calmed me down by telling me that all of this was happening as part of God's plan."

What exactly did he tell you?

"He said, 'Joseph, son of David, don't be afraid to take your wife Mary into your house—the child who has been conceived in her is from the Holy Spirit. She'll give birth to a son and you shall name him Jesus, because he'll save his people from their sins.'"

The angel called Mary your wife. It isn't clear to me—

were you engaged at that point or married?

"Our system was a little different from yours. First there was the marriage pledge, which corresponds somewhat to the engagement of today. During this period the man and woman were already considered as joined together, but they did not yet live together. The marriage pledge was binding by law and could only be broken through divorce. It was during this time that Mary received the announcement that she was going to have a child. After this first stage, the man and woman began their life together as a married couple."

And it was at the beginning of this stage that you went to Bethlehem?

"Yes, because of the census that was ordered by Rome. Bethlehem was my family's place of origin. Mary did not have to come with me, but we felt it was best under the circumstances. It was a very tiring trip that lasted four days. We had to cross the plain of Esdraelon, pass through inhospitable Samaria, and push on through the hills of Judea."

What did you think when the men from the East arrived with their gifts?

"I understood very little of what they said. They spoke a strange language, which I had never heard before. I don't even know what their names were. Perhaps they were wise men from Persia, or from Arabia. Maybe they were astronomers. Who knows?"

They say that these wise men followed a star?

"Yes. Many astronomers have tried to identify that star. Some thought it was what people later called Haley's comet. But that star was a miraculous event, outside the normal happenings in the heavens."

When the angel told you about the danger in Bethlehem, why did you decide to flee to Egypt?

"We Hebrews had always considered Egypt a place of refuge. It was there that the victims of persecution went to stay. We went there when our land was struck with famine. From the time of Nebuchadnazzar a large Jewish community had formed there. But our stay in Egypt was brief. After Herod died, the angel came to me a third time to tell me that the danger to Jesus' life had passed. We went back to Galilee and settled in Nazareth."

What was Nazareth like?

"It was a small village with very few houses, most of them inside the caves on the hillsides. The landscape was very beautiful. People worked in the fields and were poor. There was also a little synagogue."

Back then were young people different than they are now?

"They lived differently because the society was different. But they were the same as young people today, although maybe a little less clever."

What was Jesus like?

"He was a boy like the others, with a vibrant, ready intelligence. He was very curious. I taught him what I knew about our religion. He always wanted to know more, and he would run down to the synagogue to learn. He grew up first at his mother's side and then at my side. He helped me with my work, and in a very short time became an excellent carpenter."

What did they teach him in the synagogue?

"For us Hebrews, the synagogue was the "common house." People went there to listen to the word of God and to organize their community life. In the synagogue controversies were resolved and children were taught. The rabbi read the law and told stories from the Old Testament, which the children memorized so that they could teach them to their children."

Joseph, you were a hidden figure, connected to Mary, always ready to help and protect her. Are you satisfied with your life?

"I would have to say yes. God gave me everything. I loved Jesus and Mary very deeply. There were things that amazed me and that I couldn't explain. As when we lost Jesus in the holy city and found him at the temple. After Mary scolded him, he simply said that he had to concern himself with 'his' father's things. What did he mean? However, at the time I was happy just to have found him."

Why did you go to Jerusalem?

"All Hebrews had to make a pilgrimage to the temple, at least once a year, for one of the three principal festivals: Passover, which was in the spring; Pentecost, which was in the summer; or the Feast of Booths, which was in the fall."

Did Jesus go to Jerusalem every year?

"The first time we brought him to the temple was when he was

HOW MANY PEOPLE LIVED IN THE HOLY LAND?

Jesus was born in Bethlehem of Judea rather than in Nazareth because of a census that the Romans ordered. Joseph had to go to register in his family's place of origin, Bethlehem, the city of David. Mary accompanied him.

A census (the registration and cataloging of all the inhabitants of a territory) was not a new thing in the world of 2,000 years ago. The ancient Chinese, Egyptians, Babylonians, and Greeks had already used this method. And as for the Hebrews, Moses himself had all the men able to serve in the army counted by family and by tribe. Later on, for the Romans, a census was a common fact of life. During the period of the Republic, the Romans held a census every nine years. The motive was not just to count the inhabitants, but also to know how many people they could tax, call to serve in the military, etc.

But how many people lived in the holy land at the time when Jesus was born? It is calculated that the global population was around 255,000,000. The number of people in Jesus' homeland was probably around two and a half million—that is, 1% of the world population. The largest city, Jerusalem, had 100,000 inhabitants.

forty days old. When he was a child, Jesus couldn't wait to go to Jerusalem. The preparations for the trip often lasted many days, in a festive atmosphere. When he was older, he used to go to Jerusalem alone."

When did Jesus start to preach?

"When I was no longer alive. I had closed my eyes for good and had joined my ancestors."

Elizabeth, the Mother of John the Baptist

"In the days of Herod, King of Judea, there was a priest named Zechariah, of the division of Abijah, and he had a wife from among the daughters of Aaron whose name was Elizabeth.... An angel of the Lord appeared to him, standing to the right of the incense altar. Zechariah was terrified when he saw him and fear fell upon him, but the angel said to him, 'Fear not, Zechariah—your petition has been heard. Your wife Elizabeth will bear you a son, and you shall name him John.'"
(Luke 1:11-13)

Would you like to introduce yourself?

"My name is Elizabeth, which means 'God has promised.' My husband, Zechariah, was a priest in the temple of Jerusalem. I was also from a priestly family. I was descended from Aaron, the first Hebrew priest and Moses' brother. Mary the mother of Jesus was my relative, although she was much younger than I."

What does it mean to be the mother of a prophet?

"I don't know. The joy of having a baby was so great that I couldn't think about the meaning of the announcement that the angel made to my Zechariah."

Where did you live?

"In a small, unimportant village in the hills of Judea, five or six miles from Jerusalem. Now it is called Ain Karim. The hill was covered with red grape vines and cypress trees. It was a very peaceful village. We moved there because we were trying to escape the crowdedness of Jerusalem. I was quite old, and my husband was too. Every once in a while he would go to Jerusalem to take care of his priestly duties in the temple."

You say you were old. Why did you still want to have a child?
"It seems crazy, but I never stopped praying to God, until he made a new life blossom within me."

But didn't you realize that nature has set limits for bearing children?
"Nature has, yes, but God hasn't. I couldn't forget that other women in similar situations had had the privilege of having children, and their children had always turned out to be exceptional. Sarah, the wife of Abraham, had a son named Isaac when she was very old; Rachel, the wife of Jacob, who was considered sterile, gave birth to two children, Joseph and Benjamin. Then there was Hannah—she had been sterile too, and then she had Samuel and afterwards five other children. And Samson? A sterile woman gave birth to him, too."

But why did you want a child so badly?
"Woman is closely connected with giving and nurturing life. I felt punished and humiliated. You have to remember that I grew up among people await-ing the fulfillment of God's promises to our ancestors. Ex-pectation was part of our cul-ture. My expectation was to have a baby."

And God heard your prayers. How did that happen?
"My Zechariah was in Jerusa-lem for his priestly service. He was supposed to be there for at least two weeks. He had been chosen to offer incense in the temple (a very important and solemn function). On that day, while he was alone in the temple, God sent an angel to tell him that he would have a son and that I would no longer have the shame of sterility."

Why do you call sterility shameful?
"In Israel, a sterile woman was scorned. Tradition said that women without children were excluded from the blessing of God."

In a few words tell me what it was like to be a woman in Is-rael.
"Women worked, kept silent, and gave birth. They crushed grain with a stone and made bread; they drew water from the well; they prepared wool to make clothes; and they made sure that the lamps never ran out of oil. Women were not allowed to sit at the table with men, and they could never speak to men in the street."

Was Zechariah happy to have a son?
"Zechariah was old and tired. He had lost hope in everything. He didn't expect anything ex-cept to die. When the an-nouncement was made that he would become a father, he was filled with disbelief. For this small lack of faith he was pun-ished with the loss of speech. He couldn't talk. His lips moved, but no sound came out of his mouth. When he re-turned home, I realized right away that something incred-ible had happened. Pretty soon afterward, I realized I was pregnant."

What did you do?
"I didn't know who to tell my joyous news to. I stayed in the house for five months, and could feel my child growing. Every day I repeated the words of Rachel: 'Thus has the Lord dealt with me in the days he deigned to take away my dis-grace before men.'"

Which days were you the hap-piest?
"The three months that my cousin Mary spent with me. When she appeared at my door, the baby leaped in my womb. Mary had also received

a visit from an angel, who had told her about the birth of Jesus. She was in the same situation as I, and she didn't know who to confide in either. Together we sang a hymn of thanks to the Lord for our children who had been announced from heaven."

What was Mary like?

"She was serene. We talked about our worries, our anxieties, and our hopes. I was so old and she was so young. Both of us were expecting special babies. Both of us were part of the immense plan that the Lord was carrying out through us, an elderly woman and a young girl."

Why did you name your son John?

"God decided on the name. John means 'God is merciful,' or 'gift of God.'"

And Zechariah?

"As soon as he wrote the baby's name, his voice came back. The Spirit of God had descended on him. He began to prophesy and say incredible things."

Like what?

"Showing the baby to the frightened, amazed people, he said: 'You, child, will be called a prophet of the Most High, for

you will go before the Lord to prepare his ways.' Poor Zechariah! My man was never very courageous. But on that occasion, I saw him in a different light. Even I was scared by his words."

Tell me about your son.

"I called him the miracle baby. I knew that he would be a 'voice' that would tell all of Israel to prepare for the Messiah. He was a restless boy who couldn't wait to carry out his mission. I knew that he would be great before God and that he would lead many of the children of Israel to the Lord our God."

You know, of course, that both your son and the son of Mary died tragically.

"God granted me another favor: he called me to himself before my son and Mary's son were martyred."

What do you think of Herodias, your son's archenemy?

"She was very low, an adulteress, scorned by the people. She belonged to that dynasty that let their passions run wild. She was the granddaughter of the Herod who was responsible for slaughtering those innocent babies, and she wasn't satisfied that my son had been imprisoned by Herod Antipas. But to obtain John's death she had to wait for Herod to get drunk."

But wasn't it Salome who asked for your son's head?

"Yes, but at her mother's urging. Salome was just the instrument of her mother's revenge, a young woman who lived in the midst of vice and was insensitive to everything."

How would you like to be remembered?

"As the mother of John the Baptist."

THE THIRD TEMPLE OF JERUSALEM

The temple spoken of in the Gospel, which Jesus visited often, had been built by Herod the Great, who started the work in 19 B.C. The main building was finished about ten years later, but the Gospel of John tells us that some work on the construction was still going on during Jesus' public life.

This was the third temple of Jerusalem. The first was built by Solomon, and the second by Zerubbabel when the Jewish people returned from the Babylonian exile.

The splendid building that Herod wanted lasted only a few years: it was completely destroyed by the Romans in A.D. 70.

The temple was built on a large level area, bordered and supported by a mighty wall that surrounded the summit of the hill. At certain points this wall was more than 130 feet high.

The floor plan was similar to Solomon's but definitely more impressive. The main building was surrounded by a series of courtyards, along which ran porches or porticos. The main entrance led into the first courtyard, called the "Courtyard of the Gentiles," which everyone could enter. However, written notices were displayed prohibiting non-Hebrews from entering the next courtyard, which was called the "Courtyard of the Women." The notices stated that any pagan who would violate the prohibition and thus desecrate the holy place would be condemned to death. While Jewish women were only allowed to go as far as the second courtyard, the men were allowed to go into the third courtyard called the "Courtyard of the Israelites." At the end of this courtyard there was an area reserved for priests, a the sacrificial altar situated right in the front of the main building. The temple itself was entered by passing through a large vestibule which led into a room called the "the Holy Place." In this room was the altar of incense. At the far end of this room, separated by the "Temple Veil," was the most interior and most sacred room, called the "Holy of Holies." This room did not contain the Ark of the Covenant, as it had in Solomon's day. The Ark disappeared at the time of the Babylonian conquest.

Herod the Great, the Bloodthirsty King

"When Jesus was born in Bethlehem of Judea in the days of King Herod, behold, Magi from the east arrived in Jerusalem asking, 'Where is the newborn King of the Jews? We saw his star rising and came to worship him.' When King Herod heard this he was troubled...and absolutely furious, and he ordered the killing of all the children in Bethlehem and of all its neighborhood from two years old and younger."
(Matthew 2:1-3, 16)

Is Herod a Hebrew name?
"It's a Greek name that means 'belonging to the class of heroes.' My father, Antipas, was an Idumean. He came from the region south of Judea. My mother's name was Kufra and she was an Arab."

You were a much hated king. Why during your whole reign, did you never win the favor of the Jewish people?
"The mass of the Hebrew population at the time was un-der the influence of the Phari-sees, a class that called for ab-solute observance of the law. They did not tolerate even a minimum amount of contami-nation from other traditions. I,

on the other hand, tried to introduce the Hellenistic culture into my kingdom. I brought Greek philosophers and educated men to my court. I gave my sons a Hellenistic education. But it was also my political position that bothered them."

What was your position?
"At that time when the Romans controlled the Mediterranean, I was the 'allied king.' I was therefore under the power of Rome, but not under the Roman governor. I was obligated to defend the borders of the territory that was entrusted to me. In case of war, I had to contract auxiliary troops. In foreign policy, my decisions were subject to the approval of Rome, even though my subjects did not have to pay taxes to the empire. In the administration of internal affairs, however, I was absolutely free. It is therefore understandable that I, for example, put a Roman eagle on the door of the temple of Jerusalem. Yet the Jewish people rebuked me even for that."

A gesture of that kind did not reveal a large amount of religious sensitivity. But there was also something else: you were known to be a cruel and bloodthirsty king.

"Well, this type of behavior is true about all kings. A king cannot be weak. During the years that I was in control, I always sought to strengthen my throne. For this reason, for example, I ordered the death of Hyrcanus II, and later on, the death of my brother-in-law, Aristobulus III. Because of my birth, I could never be a high priest, but I had to make sure that no one else well liked by the people attained that position, for they might try to cap-

ture my throne. I even had to do away with my wife, my beloved Mariamne, and my sons Alexander and Aristobulus, when I heard that they had turned against me. And they were not the only ones.... It was very painful, certainly, and it condemned me to a bloody solitude surrounded by hate, but all of this was the price of power."

Is that the reason why you ordered the death of Jesus and the massacre of innocent children?

"I had many people killed. What does the life of twenty babies from Bethlehem matter? Put yourself in my shoes: I could not tolerate the fact that the wise men came to ask me where they could find the newborn "King of the Jews." Neither did I want them spreading this rumor among my subjects. I had ordered the execution of my own children to secure my throne, so I certainly was not going to bow down to a newborn of unknown origin."

Your cynicism is sickening. I'm not at all surprised that you were so hated. Yet you also did some great things.

"I certainly was not a loved king. Nevertheless, if my people had understood me and justly valued my accomplishments, my reign would be known as a period of profound peace and stability. I gave the people of Judea political stability and prosperity. I already mentioned that during my reign, the Jewish people did not pay taxes to Rome, not did they have to enlist in the Roman legions. I was also very

WHO RULED THE HOLY LAND IN BIBLICAL TIMES?

The ancient "promised land" of the Hebrews is a small region that extends about 150 miles from north to south and around 60 miles from east to west. This piece of land lies along the eastern shore of the Mediterranean Sea. The most important events for the Jewish people, at the time of Jesus and before, happened in the interior areas, especially around the Dead Sea, the Jordan River, and Lake Gennesaret (the Sea of Galilee). At the time of Jesus, the holy land had already been under Roman rule for decades. Even though initially the Hebrews ruled it themselves, it was still under Roman power. In 47 B.C., an Idumean named Antipas was selected by Julius Caesar to be the ruler of Judea. About a decade later his son, Herod the Great, obtained the title of King of the Jews from the Romans, and he reigned over the holy land until his death, around 4 B.C. The kingdom was then divided between his three sons: Archelaus, called Herod the Ethnarch, governor of Judea, Samaria and Idumea; Herod Antipas, tetrarch of Galilee and Perea; Philip, tetrarch of Iturea and Traconitis.

A decade later, Archaelaus showed he was completely incapable of ruling his territories, so in A.D. 6 the Romans removed him. Judea, Samaria, and Idumea became Roman provinces governed by a prefect or procurator who was sent by Rome and answered to the emperor. This governor was under the supervision of the imperial "legate" in the province of Syria. The fifth procurator of Judea was Pontius Pilate, who remained in power from A.D. 26 to 36. Therefore, during the years of the preaching and the death of Jesus, his homeland—while all under Roman control—was divided into three parts, one governed by the procurator Pontius Pilate, and the others by the tetrarchs Herod Antipas and Philip.

kind to them in other ways. For example in the year 728 from the foundation of Rome (25 B.C. in the modern numeration), there was a great famine in Judea. Out of my own pocket I paid for the grain that was needed to feed my subjects. As you can see, I helped my subjects, even though I did not succeed in making them love me. In fact, after the first few times they betrayed me, I had to learn to defend myself from them. This is what made their hate for me even worse."

Can you tell me more about your economic accomplishments?

"Under my reign, Judea knew a prosperity that it hadn't known since the days of King Solomon. They were thirty years of peace, of economic and commercial growth, and of protection of the culture. It was a period of construction, which also helped to create jobs. I had the old royal city of Samaria built giving it the name Sebaste in honor of the Roman emperor, Caesar Augustus. I founded the city of Caesarea, which became the residence of the Roman procurator. In Jerusalem I created a theater, an amphitheater, a hippodrome and the royal palace, surrounded by towers and a great wall. I had the temple restored,

making it larger and surrounding it with a huge wall of stone adorned with columns and doors."

In Rome they used to say it was better to be Herod's pig than Herod's child. Why?

"There are many stories about me. Do you know why they said that? Because in Israel it was forbidden to eat pork; therefore there was no danger that a pig would be killed. While my children.... But I re-

peat, I only condemned those who plotted against me behind my back."

Did you really order that all the richest citizens should be killed on the day of your death so that there would be mourning at your funeral?

"...And not the joy of a people freed from their hated ruler? It's always the same story. I was a great king of the Hebrews, and I was not even Hebrew."

John the Baptist, the Voice in the Desert

"In those days John the Baptist appeared, preaching in the desert of Judea and saying, 'Repent, for the Kingdom of Heaven has come!' He was the one Isaiah the prophet was referring to when he said, 'A voice crying out in the desert, prepare the way of the Lord, make straight his paths.'"

(Matthew 3:1-3)

John, what were your parents like?

"They were very affectionate, but very anxious. I heard my mother telling the story of my wondrous birth so many times! She and Zechariah, my father, were already old. They had lived a very sad life because they couldn't have any children. But the miracle of Sarah, wife of Abraham, was repeated in my mother. Each had a child when she was very old."

Why did you go out into the desert?

"I didn't run away from home. I loved my parents very much, We were pretty "well off," since our family was of the priestly class. But ever since I was a child, I had felt the spirit of God calling me to carry out a special mission. Then my parents died, and I was able to follow my calling in the desert of Judea. There it was clear that I had to preach about the coming of the Messiah, inviting everyone to prepare themselves with penance and conversion."

But why did you have to go into the desert?

"In my country, there was an

25

old tradition. When someone wanted to live under the 'watchful eye of God' they went into the desert for a period of time to pray and to fast. Even Jesus went into the desert for a while. Near the banks of the Dead Sea, a religious community had formed (called the Essenes). But the desert of Judea was not only a sanctuary for those who wanted to pray and meditate in solitude. A thousand years before the time of Jesus, David hid in the desert to escape the fury of Saul. And people hid in the desert at the time of the Maccabean revolt. In the desert you could find people of every type: the exiled, the persecuted, robbers and criminals."

Who were the "Essenes"?
"They considered themselves to be 'children of light,' and they regarded all others as 'children of darkness.' It was a community formed by men who lived in buildings and caves near the Dead Sea. They loved to call themselves the 'sons of light,' and they lived waiting for the final battle against the 'sons of darkness,' which they expected to win. They spent their time working and studying the Scriptures. They dressed all in white; they hated bloody sacrifices and scorned money. Among other things they preached about the sharing of goods, the prohibition of swearing, the contempt of human knowledge."

How were you able to survive in the desert?
"Self-denial doesn't bother you if you have the fire of the Spirit inside you and a mission to complete. My bed was the bare ground, my pillow, a stone. At night I lit a fire to keep myself warm and to protect myself from the wild beasts. My clothing was made of a rough piece of camel skin. My food consisted of grasshoppers, wild honey and blades of grass."

Then eventually you began to preach near the fords where people crossed the Jordan. When they asked if you were the Messiah, what did you answer?
"I said: 'I am a voice crying out in the desert: prepare the way of the Lord.' They were ancient words which the prophet Isaiah had already spoken. I cried out in the middle of the desert, but my voice had a very far reaching echo. From the

26

Jordan it bounced to the hill of Zion, where Jerusalem stood. My voice even reached Tiberias, where the adulterer Herod Antipas lived."

Why did you baptize people?
"Baptism symbolized a radical purification, a cleansing from any past mistake. It prepared people for the coming of the kingdom of God."

Did you know who the Messiah was?
"The identity of the Messiah never worried me. I knew that he was to come from God, had been announced by the prophets, and was already in the world. And I was ready to serve him. Then I realized that my cousin Jesus of Nazareth was the Messiah the day I baptized him in the Jordan River."

Had you met Jesus before?
"We were cousins and my mother talked about her cousin Mary and her son often. But they lived far from Ain Karim, where we lived. Some painters have mistakenly painted us playing together as children, but I actually only met him once—the day that I baptized him. Even though I only saw him that once, it was as though I already knew him: he was the Messiah."

What was your meeting like?
"I found myself standing face to face with him in the Jordan River. He wanted me to baptize him, but I said it was he who should have been baptizing me. Jesus signaled for me to be quiet. He looked into my eyes and said, 'We have to fulfill the plan of God.'"

And you baptized him?
"Yes. I put my hand on his shoulder and had him dip into the current. Without saying a word, Jesus went back to the river bank. At that moment the sky seemed to open and a powerful voice spoke: 'This is my beloved Son in whom I am well pleased.' It was the voice of God."

And what did you do then?
"I was stunned and stood there watching him disappear into the crowd. (The banks of the Jordan were filled with people waiting to be baptized.) But the next time I saw him, I began to tell my disciples, 'Here is the Lamb of God who takes away the sin of the world.'"

Why did Jesus have himself baptized if he had no sin?
"Certainly not to receive forgiveness, but rather to identify himself completely with human beings. By entering the water of the Jordan he took on

himself the responsibility for the sins of humanity. He accepted his human destiny and everything that went with it."

You announced that the Messiah would be an avenging judge. Isn't that in contrast with the message of Jesus?
"I was inspired by the prophets of the Old Testament. I haven't been called the last prophet for nothing. I foretold the coming of a Messiah who would save the good and punish the evil. But to tell the truth, the preaching of Jesus was on another plane. As Savior, Jesus was kind toward sinners."

What did you preach?
"I insisted that everyone could be saved through repentance—that is, they could change their lives for the better without changing their position in life. Soldiers did not need to become deserters, men in the villages did not need to isolate themselves in the desert, but everyone needed to be fair to others. Basically this is the difference between my cousin and myself: I insisted on fear of the judgment of God; Jesus proclaimed above all else the love of God for all people."

When Herod Antipas ordered your arrest, where were you taken?

"To the fortress of Machaerus, east of the Dead Sea, one of Herod's sumptuous homes. They threw me into a dungeon carved out of the rock. A long chain bound to my foot was fastened to a huge ring of steel embedded in the wall."

How did you die?
"I was beheaded."

You were killed because of the whim of a woman. Couldn't this have been avoided?

"Herodias hated me. I had declared publicly that as the wife of Philip, she had no business living as the queen of Philip's brother, Herod Antipas. But that was just the last straw. I had bothered her constantly with everything I said about living honestly and uprightly. The faith of Moses and the prophets had been corrupted throughout the land. Only the Messiah could save the chosen people and fulfill God's promises. And time was almost up, I told them. The night that Herod ordered my death he was drunk, and Herodias' daughter, Salome, looked very beautiful. Herod rashly promised to give her almost anything she asked for. Then he was stuck. He felt he couldn't go back on his word in front of all those guests...."

LIFE IN THE DESERT

John the Baptist, Jesus' forerunner and herald, was still quite young when he went to live in the desert to prepare himself for his mission. He probably lived in the desolate land near the Dead Sea. But the word "desert" can also mean a solitary peace and not necessarily a land that lacks all vegetation. In any case, "living in the desert" clearly means living a life of solitude in which a person is deprived of comforts and conveniences. It is a way of getting closer to God and preparing oneself to overcome the difficulties of life.

Before starting his public life, Jesus too, went to live in the desert for forty days. At the end of that time the devil tried to tempt him into having a comfortable life filled with triumph and power. But Jesus did not fall into the trap. He showed that prayer, fasting and penance help to make the spirit stronger than the body.

In the first centuries of Christianity, the anchorites would follow this way of life. They were people who lived alone, deprived of everything. They dedicated themselves to prayer.

What happened to Herod Antipas?
"His nephew Agrippa accused him of treason. Herod was dismissed from the government of Galilee and exiled to Gaul near the Pyrenees, where he died in the year A.D. 40. No one cried for him."

Was your work useful?
"Well, it certainly wasn't useless. I prepared people for the coming of the Messiah. I gathered a group of followers together, from whom Jesus picked some of his disciples."

Speaking about you to his disciples, Jesus said that no man born of woman was greater than you. Is that true?
"I am not even worthy enough to unfasten the straps of his sandals."

Peter, the Leader of the Apostles

"Then he asked them, 'But you—who do you say I am?' Peter replied, 'You're the Messiah, the Son of the Living God!' And in response Jesus said to him, 'Blessed are you, Simon son of Jonah, for it wasn't flesh and blood that revealed this to you, but my Father in Heaven. And now I tell you, that you are Peter, and on this rock I will build my church, and the gates of Hell will not prevail against it. I will give you the keys to the Kingdom of Heaven, and whatever you bind on earth will have been bound in Heaven, and whatever you loose on earth will have been loosed in Heaven.'"
(Matthew 16:15-19)

Peter, can you describe your people, the Hebrews?
"We were the people chosen by God to hand down faith in him and to prepare for the coming of the Messiah, who was to be the ideal leader. We weren't really aware that the Messiah was to redeem man from sin. We lived in the holy land, a small place about the size of Massachusetts, which at my time was made up of various regions: Galilee, Judea, Perea, Samaria and the Decapolis. We were under Roman rule when Jesus, the Messiah, was born."

Sincere about your weaknesses and humble about your greatness, you are one of the most loved persons in the Gospel story. Can you tell me

29

briefly about your life with Jesus?

"I was a professional fisherman before I was called by Jesus. He changed my name from Simon to Cephas; that is, Peter. I was married to a woman from Capernaum, and one day Jesus cured my mother-in-law. I loved him very much.... But how can I tell you briefly about the time I spent with him? I'll tell you quickly about a few episodes.

"One time when we were crossing Lake Tiberias, I tried to go to Jesus, who was walking on the water, but after a few steps, I sank because I had lost faith. At the Last Supper I protested because Jesus wanted to wash my feet. When he was arrested, I drew my sword and cut off the ear of one of the guards."

Which day was the worst for you?

"Naturally, the day that Jesus died, in that horrible way. And I was so ashamed that before he died, I denied him three times. He had told me beforehand that I would do it."

Where did you start preaching?

"In Judea—first in Jerusalem, then after Saul's persecution started I preached in other Judean cities and towns. We preached the Gospel to our Jewish fellow countrymen first of all."

And how was the word received?

"Very well. In the spring of the year 30, to celebrate Pentecost, a harvest feast, many people traveled to Jerusalem. I told them about Jesus' rising from the dead. They not only listened with interest, many of them asked to be baptized. I'm not sure how many people we baptized that day, but certainly more than a thousand. In the Acts, Luke says 3,000, but sometimes he tends to combine events."

Why were you afraid to be seen with Gentiles, the Christians who had come from paganism?

"Do you mean when I went to Antioch? You have to remember that I was one of the first to say that we had to preach the Gospel of Jesus, not only to the Hebrews, but also to the Gentiles. Except for Deacon Philip, I was the first to receive a Gentile into the Church—the Roman Centurion, Cornelius. Here's what happened in Antioch: Out of respect for the group of Hebrew Christians, who were following the Jewish law and not eating with non-Jews, I avoided eating with the Gentile Christians. There were many of them in Antioch. Because of my behavior Paul and I had an argument. But everything was cleared up. I must tell you it was a very useful incident, because it made us discuss some things and make changes. This helped to break the barriers that divided the Hebrews and the Gentiles."

Why did you, leader of the Apostles, decide to move to Rome?

"The capital of the Empire was a crossroads of different races, of commerce, of armed forces, and of cults. Besides the fact that Rome ruled the world, it also allowed for the assimilation of different cultures. The city had all the characteristics necessary to spread the message of Jesus. The Romans were particularly sensitive to and tolerant of religion. Many Romans—merchants, soldiers, and travelers—became Christians with enthusiasm."

What did you find in Rome?

"There was a large community of Hebrews. Many of them had already become Christians. The Christians coming from a pagan background (and these were few in comparison with the number of inhabitants in Rome) organized themselves into small groups. They gathered in private homes to pray. Even though imperial Rome was very liberal toward its citizens, the first Christians tried to keep themselves hidden. Poor people and slaves were the most open to the new religion, but there were educated, intellectual people who joined as well."

What did the Romans believe in?

"Some didn't believe in much of anything. In those years—around A.D. 60—the traditional Roman religion, based on devotion to one's ancestors and honoring the three principal divinities, Jupiter (Jove), Minerva, and Juno, was on the decline. In practice, there was space in Rome for any divinity that was dear to the people. The religious fervor had weakened. The emperors had become the true religious point of reference. Often they required acts of adoration from their subjects."

Can you tell me about the persecutions?

"The Jewish leaders were the first to persecute us: the deacon Stephen and later James, the brother of John, fell victim to their zeal. Then there was the first great Roman persecution, that of the mad, cruel

Nero. At that time the number of Christian martyrs grew every year."

On those times did you recall what Jesus said about persecution?

"Yes—especially this phrase: 'Blessed are you when they insult you and persecute you...because of me; rejoice and be glad, because your reward will be great in Heaven'" (Matthew 5:11-12).

Why did Nero order the death of the Christians?

"In July of A.D. 64, a tremendous fire broke out in Rome. Maybe Nero didn't really start it, but the fact that people immediately accused him of it shows that he was known for great cruelty. Even before trying to repair the disaster, he looked for someone he could blame for it. A Roman historian, Tacitus, confirmed this.

"Nero decided to lay the blame on a new religious sect. He didn't know anything about us. He had his men arrest every Christian they could find and condemn them to death after a summary trial. Some were thrown to the beasts, others were crucified. Others were covered with resin and burned as torches. Before this, Rome hadn't been aware of us. After, instead, people began to look at Christians with a kind of curiosity."

And you yourself—how did you die?

"I was nailed to a wooden cross upside down."

Where were you executed?

"Where the basilica named after me stands now. Certainly the executioner could not have dreamed that from my tomb would rise another empire, a spiritual one, destined to live on and on."

GALILEE, THE REGION OF JESUS

Galilee, the region in which Jesus spent most of his life, is located in the northern part of the holy land and is bordered by the plain of Jezreel or Esdraelon to the south and the Sea of Galilee to the east. There are two main sections in this region: lower Galilee, which is the hilly southern part, where the elevation is never more than 2,000 feet; and upper Galilee, which is more mountainous, with mountain tops often more than 3,200 feet above sea level. The Sea of Galilee, a lake that is about thirteen miles long and eight miles wide, was called the Sea of Kinneret or Kinarot in ancient times. At the time of Jesus it was called by different names: Lake Gennesaret, Lake of Tiberias, or the Sea of Galilee.

Galilee was crossed by many commercial roads and therefore it was more open to outside influence than Judea was. Its population was also mixed: alongside Jewish families lived people of many different nationalities. There were also many foreign travelers in the region.

The people lived mostly off the fruits of the land, which was very fertile. Besides cereal grains, they cultivated olives, figs, grapes, dates, and flax. Along the banks of Lake Gennesaret people fished and salt-cured their catch to preserve it. The disciples whom Jesus called on the banks of the lake were fisherman: Peter, Andrew, James, and John.

Andrew, the First Apostle Called

"The next day John was again standing there, as well as two of his disciples, and he looked right at Jesus as he was walking by and said, 'Here is the Lamb of God.' His two disciples heard him speaking and they followed Jesus.... Now Andrew, the brother of Simon Peter, was one of the two who were listening to John and had followed him. He first found his own brother, Simon, and said to him, 'We've found the Messiah!'— which translated, is 'Christ.' He led him to Jesus."

(John 1:35-37, 40-42)

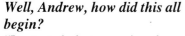

Well, Andrew, how did this all begin?

"It started that morning long ago on the banks of the Jordan River. I was there to watch the prophet John baptizing people. I spent hours on the banks of the Jordan listening to the words of the prophet. I was there when a voice came from heaven which said: 'This is my beloved son.' I was there when John said: 'This is the Lamb of God.'"

The Gospels say that when the voice spoke a dove circled in the sky. Is that true?

"I didn't see a dove. The description of the evangelists could be figurative. The dove was a symbol in Israel; it reminded us of salvation. It was a dove that signaled to Noah that the punishment had ended and that life had come back to the earth. Of course, for Christians the dove also symbolizes the Holy Spirit."

What amazed you about John the Baptist?

"His forceful voice. The words came out of his thin face with an amazing strength. People were amazed and frightened by him. I watched him and listened to him for hours. He often cried out, even when he was in the middle of the river."

And what did he say?

"'The time has come when the axes will be laid at the root of every tree: every tree that does not bear fruit will be cut down and thrown in the fire.' John didn't advise extraordinary things. He simply called for the practice of charity and honesty in doing one's duty. When he was asked, 'What should we do?' he replied: 'Let whoever has two tunics share with the one who has none, and let whoever has food do likewise.' Once, some tax collectors came to him on the banks of the river. He said to them: 'Collect nothing more than what has been designated for you.' Everyone asked him what to do. When he was with a group of soldiers, he said: 'Don't rob or cheat anyone,

and be satisfied with your wages.'"

What year was this?

"It was the fifteenth year of Tiberias' reign; Pontius Pilate was governing Judea; Herod Antipas was the tetrarch of Galilee and his brother Philip was the tetrarch of Iturea and Traconitis, while Lysanias governed the province of Abilene. It was the year A.D. 28."

Can you describe the Jordan River to me?

"It is a witness of the history of my people. It's not impressive like the Nile: it's only 200 miles long. It starts at 490 feet above sea level in the Anti-Lebanon mountains, gathering the water from the brooks that run down Mount Hermon. It flows south for about twenty-five miles, as the raven flies, and rushes down a gorge into the Sea of Galilee. Within sixteen miles, by the way, the Jordan descends from 223 feet above sea level to 696 feet below. Leaving Lake Gennesaret the river twists and turns until it finally ends up in the salty, lifeless waters of the Dead Sea, 1,290 feet below sea level."

When did you become one of Jesus' disciples?

"At the time I mentioned. I was

the first to be called. I asked Jesus where he was staying, and he said, 'Come and see.' Then I told my brother that I had found the Messiah. We spent a few days with Jesus then. Later, I was in a boat on the shore of Lake Gennesaret and Jesus appeared, again to 'call' me and my brother."

Your name, Andrew, is Greek. Why do you have a Greek name?

"It's not that surprising. The Greeks and their culture were all around us. But very little of Greek culture was adopted by the Jewish people—except for Greek names, such as Andrew, Philip, Stephen and Paul. Latin names were also popular, such as: Rufo, Anthony and Niger."

What were you like? Can you tell me an episode from your life with Jesus?

"I was very quiet and was reverentially afraid of him. I didn't dare interrupt when he spoke. I tried to understand the meaning of his words, but it wasn't easy. For example, once he told Philip that we ought to feed a hungry crowd. We were in the mountains. Night was falling and there were people everywhere. They were all hungry. I tried to be helpful and told Jesus that one child there had five loaves of bread and two fish. It was then that he worked the miracle of the multiplication of bread and fish."

How many people were fed?
"Around 5,000 men, not counting the women and children. When we collected the leftovers, they filled twelve baskets."

Did you understand who Jesus was?
"His true nature always escaped me, as it did everyone else. There was no doubt that he was sent by God. But we weren't able to free ourselves from the idea that the Messiah would be a conqueror. Not even Peter, John and James, who knew more than I did because they were present at the transfiguration, understood completely who Jesus really was. We believed he was the Messiah, but we still thought we would have to fight with our swords to establish his kingdom. In fact some of us were so sure of it, that we had gotten swords for ourselves."

Can you tell me about some "wonders" of your land?
"The temple, which may well have been more imposing than that of Solomon himself; the monastery of the "Essenes" near the Dead Sea; the Sea of

Galilee, which is excellent for fishing; and Tiberias, the new city which the Jewish people considered impure, which was built by order of Herod Antipas."

What were some of the stories from the Bible that fascinated you when you were a child?
"In our times the Bible was handed on orally. Our parents told us stories which they had

learned from the rabbis in the synagogue. Which stories fascinated me the most? The great flood, the tower of Babel, the 'fairy-tale' life of Ruth, who wanted to join our people and worship our God; the friendship between David and Jonathan; Daniel in the lion's den; the story of Abraham at the moment when he about to sacrifice his son Isaac; and finally the passage through the Jordan River."

And now, coming back to Christianity, why did Christians take the cross as their emblem—an instrument of torture?

"The first Christians didn't choose the cross. The first Christian symbols were bread and fish and the image of the good shepherd. Only later on was the cross selected, when people understood its value as the instrument of our redemption."

You yourself died on a cross, I understand.

"That's what has been said about me for centuries, and I won't comment on it. The most popular story about my death says that I was crucified in Greece on a cross that had the form of an X. For that reason that type of cross is called 'the cross of St. Andrew.'"

THE JORDAN RIVER

The Jordan is the principal river of the holy land. It runs from north to south. Originating from four streams fed by melting snows from Mt. Hermon, the Jordan passes through a cultivated area (the former Lake Huleh) and plunges down a steep gorge to Lake Gennesaret (also called the Sea of Galilee). This lake, about thirteen miles long and eight wide, with a maximum depth of 230 feet, was formed in a tectonic depression—that is, a depression resulting from shifts in the earth's crust. The whole Jordan Valley with the Dead Sea and the Gulf of Aqaba are located on a great geological fault. The surface of the lake is 696 feet below sea level.

After flowing out of the lake, the Jordan continues south until it reaches the Dead Sea, situated 1,290 feet below sea level. The distance between Lake Gennesaret and the Dead Sea is only about sixty-five miles by air, but the river winds so much that it's actually more than two hundred miles long. The valley near the banks of the river is filled with dense vegetation, but the cliffs that surround the Dead Sea are barren rock.

The Jordan ends at the Dead Sea, for this large lake has no outlet. Being so far below sea level, the Dead Sea is warm, and water evaporates from its surface rapidly. Therefore, this lake of fifty-three by ten miles has a very high salt content—around 26% as against the ocean's average of 3.5%. This high salt content makes it impossible for any vegetation or fish to survive.

The cross of St. Andrew forms part of many insignias. It's also part of the British flag. Can you explain this?

"Maybe it's so popular because I was the first apostle to follow Jesus."

James, Son of Thunder

"Now as he was walking along the sea he saw two brothers—Simon, who is called Peter, and his brother Andrew—casting a throw net into the sea—they were fishermen. And he said to them, 'Follow me, and I'll make you fishers of men!' So they left their nets at once and followed him. As he continued on from there he saw two more brothers, James son of Zebedee and his brother John, who were in the boat with their father Zebedee mending their nets, and he called them. So they left the boat and their father at once and followed him."
(Matthew 4:18-22)

Would you like to introduce yourself?
"My name is James, which is a form of Jacob, and I grew up in the important center of Capernaum, in Galilee. My fa-

FISHING IN THE LAKE OF GENNESARET

The Gospels often mention fish and fishing. In fact, fish was one of the most important foods for the Jewish people.

Some fishing was done in the Jordan River and perhaps also along the Mediterranean coast; however, the holy land had almost no natural harbors.

Most of the fish, therefore, came from Lake Gennesaret (the Sea of Galilee). There were nine fishing villages along the lake. They included: Bethsaida, Capernaum, Gennesaret, Magdala and Tiberias. This last village was built in the time of Jesus; in fact it was founded by Herod Antipas, son of Herod the Great. It was called Tiberias in honor of the Roman emperor Tiberius.

Jewish fishermen sometimes fished with hooks made of bone or steel, but they usually preferred nets—either throwing them by hand from the shore or trailing them behind their boats.

ther, Zebedee, had a flourishing fish business there, with many workers. When Jesus called me, we left everything and followed him."

Why did you say "we"?
"Because my brother John was there too. Our father gave us his blessing. Our mother, Salome, was very emotional and couldn't help crying. Our mother was always close to us. Whenever she found out that we were near Capernaum, she would come to see us. She never got tired of listening to Jesus."

What kind of fish were there in Lake Gennesaret?
"The same kinds that are there now. The most important was the kind that people today call 'the fish of St. Peter.'"

Could you share one or two of your memories of Jesus?
"Jesus used to call John and me *boanerges*, which means 'sons of thunder.' We were both passionate, genuine and open. And very impulsive. Once I asked Jesus to punish the Samaritans because they weren't hospitable. Jesus said I didn't know what I was saying. Another time I told him that my brother and I wanted to sit at his right hand and his left in his kingdom. Our mother

Salome supported our request. Jesus said he couldn't grant it—that it wasn't up to him...."

Was Jesus affectionate toward you?
"I was one of his favorites, with Peter, and especially John, the youngest of the group. Jesus wanted me to witness the transfiguration, the raising of Jairus' daughter and his agony in the garden of Gethsemane."

After you received the Holy Spirit, where did you go to preach?
"I traveled around Judea and Samaria. Do you know what was hardest in the beginning? People made fun of my Galilean accent."

You were the first apostle to die a martyr's death. Where and when did it happen?

"I was beheaded in Jerusalem in A.D. 42. Herod Agrippa ordered my execution."

Who was Herod Agrippa?
"He was the grandson of Herod the Great and son of Aristobulus. His father, uncle and grandmother had all been murdered by Herod the Great. Like many other eastern princes, he spent his youth in Rome making friends with Caligula and Claudius. Caligula, who became emperor after Tiberius, made Herod Agrippa a king, assigning to him the territory which was previously governed by his uncle, Philip. When another uncle, Herod Antipas, was disgraced, Herod Agrippa became the ruler of Galilee also. After Claudius became emperor, Agrippa was given control of Samaria and Judea. This meant that he ruled the same lands

that Herod the Great had ruled during his reign."

Why did Herod Agrippa want you dead?
"Agrippa was careful to respect the traditions of the Pharisees, so he became very hostile to Christians. Peter was supposed to be killed, too, but he miraculously escaped from prison."

Herod Agrippa himself died soon afterward. How did that happen?
"I'll tell the story as the historian Josephus tells it. Agrippa called for a great festival to celebrate one of Claudius' military victories. For the occasion he put on a suit made of silver. His people cheered for him, 'calling him a god.' And the king was very happy to be so well loved. But at that moment he saw an owl, the omen of funerals. He began to have severe abdominal pains and died five days later. It was the year A.D. 44."

Your death is recorded in the Bible. But what do we know about the other apostles?
"No one knows much about most of them. This shouldn't be surprising, since for the believer, glory isn't what the world expects it to be. But Christians haven't always been

happy with this uncertainty about the apostles. Because of this they've tried to reconstruct a little, imagine a little, and invent a little what written history doesn't tell us. This is how the legends started...."

Is there a legend about you?
"Yes. My legend says that when I was on my way to execution, I had time to convert the guard who was accompanying me."

Are there legends about all the apostles?

"There are some historically factual accounts, as well as stories that may be true and some that are clearly legends. You see, each of the churches from which the message of Jesus spread wanted the honor of having an apostle as founder. If Rome could boast of Peter, other cities boast of other people who were very close to Jesus. Then it became necessary to contrast the accomplishments of the apostles with those of the pagan gods. So the apostles became heroes. The legends tell of many great deeds and miracles performed by the apostles. Some of these may have been true; others were too incredible and inappropriate to believe, such as baptizing a lion and other animals."

Since you were the first apostle to die for your faith in Jesus, could you tell us about the others?

"Well, first of course, there was Peter—first in rank, I mean. He died in Rome and was buried on Vatican Hill. That's definite. His bones have been there from the beginning and people have gone there through the centuries to pray at or near his remains. Then there was James the Just, of Jerusalem. There is an historical source for the account of his death. Flavius Josephus tells us that James was stoned to death by order of the high priest. So that's definite, too. What isn't clear is whether James the Just is the same person as the apostle called 'James of Alpheus.' I know the answer of course. But I want to leave that as a challenge for scholars...."

I'll respect your wishes, of course. But that still leaves several more apostles, even though I've interviewed Andrew already. Could you tell me what is said about the other apostles?

"According to legend, Bartholomew was skinned alive and then crucified in Armenia. Thomas was killed by a spear in India. Matthew, the evangelist, had gone to Egypt to witness to his faith. It seems he was attacked and beaten to death while celebrating the Lord's Supper (the Eucharist, in other words). For Jude Thaddeus there are differing legends: one says that he went to Beirut to preach and was clubbed to death. Others say that he was killed by a sword or an axe. For centuries he was neglected because he had the same name as the traitor (Judas Iscariot, who committed suicide). For this reason Jude Thaddeus was not well liked in many countries. But he has always been very popular in Poland: Thaddeus is one of the most widespread names in that country. Simon, it is said, was cut in half in Persia...."

Let me interrupt a minute. Why does a person give up his or her life in preference to giving up the Christian religion?

"It's all a matter of values. Heaven is worth any price because it's everlasting happiness with God. To give up one's faith is to risk losing heaven. I say 'risk,' because God is merciful and may give a person another chance. But the bottom line is: when you've grown to really love Jesus and his Father, you can't bear to do anything that will harm your relationship with them...."

I understand. It's basically a matter of love, then—which is the strongest force in the world. Thank you. Who's left?

"There were also Philip, Matthias, and my brother John. Philip died during the persecution of Diocletian: he was crucified upside down, like Peter. Matthias, it seems, was stoned and then struck with an axe. John lived so long that rumors spread that he would never die. He, too, was persecuted during the reign of Diocletian, but they didn't manage to kill him. When they threw him into a cauldron of boiling oil, he came out unharmed. As far as anyone knows, he died of old age on the island of Patmos."

One last question, James: why are you the patron saint of Spain?

"A legend spread by Isidore of Seville says that I preached the Gospel there. According to tradition, my remains are buried in Santiago de Campostella which, since the eleventh century, has been the most famous place of Christian pilgrimage after the sites of the holy land."

John, the Beloved Disciple

"Now standing by Jesus' cross were his mother and his mother's sister, Mary the wife of Clopas, and Mary Magdalen. When Jesus saw his mother and the disciple he loved standing by he said to his mother, 'Woman, here is your son.' Then he said to the disciple, 'Here is your mother.' And from that hour the disciple took her into his home."
(John 19:25-27)

How much of the New Testament did you write?
"Directly or indirectly I'm connected with the Gospel that bears my name, three letters and the *Book of Revelation*."

You were called Jesus' beloved disciple; why?
"I was one of the first four disciples called by the Teacher. The others were Peter, Andrew, and my brother James. I was the youngest of the four. Perhaps that's the reason."

Weren't the other disciples jealous?
"Yes—there was some jealousy, as there is in any family."

By the way, what does "disciple" mean?
"It means a follower who is a learner or pupil."

Your Gospel is more difficult to understand than those of Mark, Matthew and Luke. Were you better educated than the others?

"No, absolutely not. I was a fisherman, just like my father Zebedee and his father. But my Gospel was written after I had lived a long time and experienced many things. My disciples and I did much reflecting before my Gospel was written. We tried to use a language suitable for the most advanced culture at the time, the Hellenistic culture—which originated with the Greeks."

What is the central point of your discussion?

"That Jesus is the Messiah, the true center of human history. He is the Son of God, revealer of the Truth. And he is the Life. I never tired of repeating that God is love and that, following his example, the true disciples of Jesus should love one another."

Isn't this an unusual teaching?

"Is it strange to preach love? And to announce hope to people, who after the sacrifice of Christ are free and equal before God? If this message is strange, then, yes, my message is unusual."

Who is the woman described in Revelation, who is clothed with the sun and has a crown of twelve stars, with the moon under her feet?

"She is a symbol of the people of God from whom the Messiah was born. But she also represents Mary, the mother of Jesus, as well as the Church, persecuted in her children."

What did the mother of Jesus mean to you?

"She was like my second mother from the moment that Jesus entrusted her to me from the cross."

Did Jesus say anything to you at the Last Supper, when you laid your head against his chest?

"He helped me understand the meaning of love until death, and what betrayal is."

Do the Gospels tell us everything that Jesus did?

"There are many other things that Jesus did, but if each of them were written down, the world could not hold all the books that would be needed."

In the four Gospels, there are many stories that don't seem to match. For example, you mention five trips that Jesus made to Jerusalem, and the other evangelists mention only one. Who is right?

"The others are only concerned about one of the journeys, the last one, which was the most important. They are more interested in religious meanings and pay little attention to the order of events."

Then the events in the Gospels didn't always take place in the order in which they are told?

"We evangelists weren't reporters, so we did not write things down after each event. We wrote after the passion and the resurrection, the two events that offered us the key to understanding the events that had taken place before. And when we told the stories we kept in mind what came afterward. This is important to remember:

when we wrote about the life of Jesus, we already knew that he had died and was raised. For this reason we added particular details that are not an exact chronicle of the events as they took place, but are intended to

THE BOOKS OF THE NEW TESTAMENT

The Bible is not simply one book, but a collection of books written at different times. It comprises seventy-three books in all, divided into two large sections: the Old Testament (forty-six books) and the New Testament (twenty-seven books).

Of the twenty-seven books in the New Testament the most important ones are the four Gospels (Matthew, Mark, Luke and John), which are basically historical. They tell us about the life and teachings of Jesus Christ. The fifth book, the *Acts of the Apostles*, is also basically historical. It narrates events from the lives of the followers of Jesus—particularly Peter and Paul—who spread the Good News (the Gospel of Christ) first in Jerusalem, then in neighboring regions and eventually far beyond.

The next twenty-one books are letters written by the apostles and other early writers to various Christian communities. Several of these are from St. Paul and people who were close to him. Others bear the names of James, John, Peter and Jude. No author is given for the Letter to the Hebrews.

The last book of the New Testament is a prophetic work called the *Book of Revelation*. It was written around the end of the first century by a certain John, who was in exile on the island of Patmos. This book contains a series of visions or revelations that were probably intended to encourage Christians in time of persecution.

symbolize or hint at what happened later."

The Gospels mention Jesus' brothers and sisters. But wasn't he an only child?

"'Brother' had a much broader

meaning for us. In the *Book of Genesis,* for example, they say, that Lot was Abraham's 'brother,' while in reality Lot was his nephew. Laban is called Jacob's 'brother,' while he was actually his uncle."

Among the apostles, you were the only eye-witness to the crucifixion. Who else was at Calvary?

"Jesus' mother was there, as I've mentioned. Then there were: my mother, Salome; the wife of Clopas, who was also named Mary; and Mary Magdalene. Besides our little group there were also occasional passers-by who challenged Jesus to save himself. They shouted: 'Save yourself and we will believe you.' Some of the members of the Sanhedrin also shouted: 'If you are the Messiah, show us by saving yourself!' And then, of course, there were the soldiers, who were playing dice."

Why didn't Jesus save himself with a miracle?

"It was no longer a question of persuading people with miracles. They had already called his previous miracles 'works of the devil.' But in actuality he was performing his greatest miracle, that of saving the human race."

I've heard that while Jesus was on the cross, he spoke seven times. Can you repeat what he said?

"The first time he spoke was to his Father. He said: 'Father, forgive them, for they don't know what they're doing.' And this surprised the people because they expected him to scream obscenities, as condemned men usually did. The second thing he said was addressed to the condemned man on his right. The thief admitted that he deserved to be punished. He recognized that Jesus was the Messiah, and he asked Jesus to remember him in heaven. Jesus replied: 'You'll be with me in Paradise.' Beneath the cross there were also people suffering. Among them was Jesus' mother, Mary. Jesus turned to her and, indicating me, he said: 'Woman, here is your son.' Then he said to me: 'Here is your mother.'"

When did he say these words?

"Around noon when the shadows were darkening. At around three in the afternoon, he spoke again. Actually, he cried out: 'My God, my God, why have you abandoned me?' It was not a cry of desperation but of suffering. It's the first line of Psalm 22, which seems to have foretold that very moment."

And the fifth time Jesus spoke?

"He said only two words: 'I'm thirsty.' A soldier took a sponge, dunked it in sour wine and wet Jesus' lips."

Sour wine?

"In hot climates, like ours, soldiers and farmers used to carry a drink that the Romans called *posca.* It was vinegar diluted with water, and it would take away your thirst quickly. Jesus had already refused to drink regular wine mixed with myrrh, because he didn't want to lessen his pain. After he had wet his lips with the vinegar, he said: 'All has been fulfilled.' This wasn't actually the end. But it tells us that Jesus had fulfilled God's promise of salvation for his people."

And his last words?

"The last words of Jesus were taken from Psalm 31, which is a prayer of trust: 'Father, into your hands I entrust my spirit.' At that point he hung his head and died."

When was your Gospel written?

"Toward the year 100, when I was very old. All of my friends who had followed Jesus had already died. As far as I know, I was the last living eye-witness."

Philip, the Fifth Apostle

"Jesus said to [Thomas], 'I am the way and the truth and the life. No one comes to the Father except through me....' Philip said to him, 'Lord, show us the Father and we'll be satisfied.' Jesus said to him, 'Have I been with you so long and yet you don't recognize me, Philip? Whoever has seen me has seen the Father! How can you say, "Show us the Father"? Don't you believe that I am the Father and the Father is in me?'"
(John 14:8-10)

Before you became an apostle, what did you do?
"I was a fisherman, like Andrew, Simon Peter, James and John. I lived in Bethsaida, a little village of fishermen on the banks of Lake Gennesaret."

Is that the same lake called Tiberias?

"Yes. It began to be called that when Herod Antipas had a city constructed on the southwest shore of the lake and named it after the emperor. The lake took the name of the city, even though many people continued to call it Lake Gennesaret or the Sea of Galilee."

Can you describe the city of Tiberias to me?
"We didn't go there very willingly. It was constructed on top of the ruins of an old cemetery, so this made the city 'impure' for us. Many foreigners and the Hebrews who were less religious lived there. It was just like a rich, immoral Greek city."

What was Lake Tiberias like?
"It was a whimsical lake, capable of sudden, violent storms; sometimes it was overflowing with fish and at other

times you could go a whole night without catching anything. It's almost 700 feet below the level of the Mediterranean Sea, so the weather can get quite warm in the summer. It's not very big—about thirteen miles long and at its widest point about eight miles across. In a boat, with the right wind, you could cross the lake in a half hour. In the rainy season the water could rise more than thirty feet in a few days."

Can you tell what a fisherman's day was like?
"Most of the day was spent in the boat. When you returned to shore, you had to separate the fish into different categories by quality and throw out all the fish that were considered impure."

Which fish were considered impure?
"Catfish, eels and lamphreys. Some fisherman would put aside their religious convictions and sell these fish to non-Hebrews. In our village the fishermen had a cooperative, and we sold our fish to the wholesalers in Jerusalem."

The first Christians chose a fish as their symbol. Why?
"Because the word 'fish' in Greek is *ichthus*. The letters of this word make an acronym in Greek for 'Jesus Christ, son of God, Savior.' This fish became a sort of code symbol during times of persecution."

Why were you, an uneducated fisherman, chosen by Jesus to be an apostle?
"I could say that it was because I had a pure heart, but that would be presumptuous. I'd prefer to answer with a phrase you have heard many times: 'The ways of the Lord are mysterious and unsearchable.'"

How was it possible for people like you to abandon their homes, their work and their families to follow someone who had called them?
"It's not a miracle. These things happen today, too. Every day someone leaves behind comfort, position and a 'good life,' to face the unknown. People are more disposed to seek the 'true life' than we think. And Jesus' call to us came when we already knew him; we had heard him many times. The Gospels relate the actual event. But there were intermediate steps. For example, before the 'call,' I had spoken about Jesus and his words many times with my friend Bartholomew from Cana."

Was it peaceful—your life with Jesus?
"Hardly—at least, not most of the time. There were crowds, miracles, journeys, days of preaching, hostile attitudes and a sense of impending danger. We were all somewhat worn out by the end."

And at the moment of his supreme sacrifice, didn't most of you betray him, at least in a certain sense?
"It's true that we weren't there with him. As a turtle hides in his shell, we took refuge in a locked room, afraid that we'd be killed too. We huddled there in fear and sorrow."

How long did you stay there?
"Several days—except when someone really needed to go out. But on the third day—according to our way of counting—something unexpected happened. Mary Magdalene arrived with strange news: 'I have seen the Lord.' We didn't believe her. He himself had to come and breathe the Holy Spirit into us. Only then did we see him in his real identity: Jesus, the Risen One."

What did Jesus say to you?
"He said he had come to bring us his peace. It was a standard greeting, but the way he said it gave it a new meaning. And then he gave us the power to forgive sins."

What does it mean to be disciples of Jesus?

"It means struggle, sacrifice—even martyrdom, although it might be only the martyrdom of facing an ironic smile or some ridicule. A real disciple spreads the Good News by his or her dedicated Christian life. To use a beautiful phrase coined by one of the saints: we'll have plenty of time to rest after we die."

What qualities did Jesus seem to admire most in people?

"Faith, and readiness to do the will of God."

Are people condemned if they don't believe?

"That's in the Gospels. However, the Gospels also remind us that God didn't send his Son to judge and condemn us but to save us. He wants everyone to come to know the truth. Many people sincerely look for the truth. But I do feel sorry for those who don't want to believe, who close their eyes to the light, who turn their backs on the truth, who prefer evil to good."

When you went out to spread the Good News, what country did you find the most fascinating?

"You might ask Paul that one. He traveled more than the rest of us."

THE WORK OF ARTISANS

The Hebrews had high regard for the work of artisans, such as blacksmiths, carpenters, tailors and shoemakers. Since Joseph, the husband of Mary and legal father of Jesus, had a carpentry shop, he was probably esteemed and respected.

Certain trades, however, were not favorably regarded. Weavers, for example, were scorned because they dedicated themselves to "women's work." Tanners were not respected because their work was considered "unclean."

The trade of potter was important, even though at Jesus' time the best ceramics probably came from neighboring lands. A potter had to have a tank of water, a potter's wheel for molding the clay, and a furnace for firing the ceramics. Hebrew potters did not varnish their products, but sometimes decorated them very simply with a red or black stripe at the top. The most popular ceramic objects were those that were necessary in everyday life: bowls of different sizes that were used for cooking, for serving food and for drinking; oil lamps; *amphoras* (two-handled jars used to carry wine or oil); small jugs to hold perfume; and other objects, including little toy statues of different animals.

Do you remember the most beautiful day, and the worst?

"The most beautiful day was when Jesus appeared in the middle of that locked room and we realized that he was truly alive. The worst was three days before—when Jesus was nailed to the cross...and I hadn't yet fully understood who he was...."

If today you had to decide where to go and preach the word of God, what country would you choose?

"I'd like to go to the countries where religion was restricted for so many years, to speak of a baby named Jesus, born in a grotto in Bethlehem, a hidden village in the hills of Judea...."

Bartholomew, the Man from Cana

"Jesus saw Nathanael coming toward him and said about him, 'Here's a true Israelite, in whom there's no guile.' Nathanael said to him, 'Where do you know me from?' Jesus answered and said to him, 'Before Philip called you, while you were under the fig tree, I saw you.' Nathanael answered him, 'Rabbi, you're the Son of God, you're the king of Israel!'"
(John 1:47-49)

Three evangelists, Matthew, Mark and Luke, place you among the apostles. Instead, on John's list the name 'Nathanael' appears instead, of 'Bartholomew.' Could you clear up this mystery for me?
"Nathanael is my real name and it means 'gift of God.' It's the name my parents gave me when I was born. Bartholomew is a 'patronymic,' which is a name formed from the father's name. It means 'son of Tolmai.' Tolmai was my father. In Israel, patronymics were common."

How did you meet Jesus?

"It was my friend Philip who told me about him. He told me that Jesus was an exceptional man and that I should meet him. He insisted so much, that I decided to come along and see for myself if he was everything Philip said he was. Jesus and I talked for a while. I have to admit that I had my doubts at first. But then I came to realize that I was face to face with a truly extraordinary person."

What did Jesus say to you?

"He said that I was a sincere, loyal Israelite."

And how did you respond to that?

"I decided to follow him."

Where were you from originally?

"I lived in Cana, a village about seven miles from Nazareth."

Is that where Jesus changed water into wine?

"Yes. There was a wedding banquet and Jesus had been invited. He brought several of us with him. Jesus' mother was there, too, giving a hand to the women of the house. At a certain point, Mary went over to her son and told him that there was no more wine."

Was it important to have wine on the table?

"Definitely. When someone was getting married, the family made severe sacrifices for months and months. Everything had to be done according to protocol. If by chance something was missing, it was a tragedy for the family and the newlyweds. In fact, the event would be sarcastically commented on in the village for years."

What did Jesus do?

"He asked the servants to fill six big stone jars with water. Then he told them to take some out and bring it to the head steward. After tasting it, the steward said to the bridegroom, 'Everyone first puts out the good wine, then when they're drunk, the lesser wine; you've kept the good wine until now.' This was Jesus' first miracle."

All the Hebrews were waiting for the Messiah. How did they picture him?

"The Zealots, the 'freedom fighters,' saw him as a liberator—an enemy of the Romans. The Essenes imagined a final kingdom led by three key figures: a prophet, a 'Messiah of Aaron' (a priest) and a 'Messiah of Israel' (a king). The Pharisees saw the Messiah as a virtuous and severe ruler capable of imposing strict laws on everyone, including Gentiles. The Sadducees, who had great political advantages in my country at that time, especially feared the arrival of a revolutionary, who would overthrow the established order...."

Why did Jesus wait till he was thirty to begin to reveal himself as the Messiah?

"At that time, thirty years represented full maturity. People weren't really listened to until they were thirty. Authority increased with age, and years were considered a guarantee of wisdom. At the gates of Jerusalem, the men who had to settle disputes were the elders—that is, people qualified by their age, not by their education."

What was Jesus like?

"He was gentle when he would urge us not to be afraid. Right after that, though, he would change his tone of voice and make us understand that we must never be lazy or half-hearted."

What do you think about Judas?

"He's portrayed in history as the traitor, the one who got Jesus arrested. He set into motion that ugly chain of events that ended on Golgatha. I'm pretty sure of this: Judas didn't understand what Jesus preached. He thought he had found a lion, when instead he had found a lamb. Judas' character may have been defamed a little too much; we haven't paid much attention to his hesitation before the betrayal and his remorse afterward. The crime he committed was enormous, it's true, but in a certain sense we all betrayed Jesus with our hiding and denials. Fortunately, the rest of us corrected ourselves. Not Judas, though. He added the sin of despair to that of betrayal by taking his own life."

What was the Hebrews' most important prayer?

"It was called the *Shemá,* which is from the first word of the text. It means 'Listen.' The *Shemá* is a prayer that Jesus himself recited many times. You'll find it in the *Book of Deuteronomy,* chapter 6. I'll recite part of it for you: 'Israel, remember this! The Lord—and the Lord alone—is our God. Love the Lord your God with all your heart, with all your soul, and with all your strength. Never forget these commands that I am giving you today. Teach them to your children. Repeat them when you are at home and when you are

away, when you are resting and when you are working. Tie them on your arms...as a reminder.... Write them on the doorposts of your houses and on your gates....'"

Bartholomew, what is charity?
"It's one of the fundamental virtues of the Christian, the one which obliges you to love God and your neighbor."

And what is true wealth?
"Certainly not what's accumulated on earth—wealth that's bound to disappear. Real treasures are those which are accumulated in heaven."

In the Sistine Chapel in Rome, Michelangelo portrayed you holding your own skin in your left hand.
"That's how he wanted to remind everyone about my martyrdom. The story is told that in Armenia, in the city of Albanopolis, I converted a king. That didn't please certain powerful persons and they condemned me to death. After being skinned alive, I was crucified."

Is it possible to imagine a more horrible death than yours?
"Persecution is always horrible. But the worst torment is

FARMING IN THE HOLY LAND

When the Israelites entered the promised land, each family was assigned some territory. But the climate and the type of soil could make farming very difficult, especially in certain parts of the country. The farmers often had to deal with droughts and with strong winds that carried the dry soil away.

In the holy land, it rains only in the winter, and there are no important rivers in the region except for the Jordan, which winds back and forth in a hot valley far below sea level. Therefore, the Hebrews were always concerned about access to wells and springs. Lack of water was a problem for everyone—city dwellers, villagers and especially farmers.

As a result, Hebrew farmers raised crops that didn't need to be irrigated—for example, barley, wheat, flax, grapes and olives. In smaller quantities they also grew legumes and greens. The most common fruits (besides grapes) were figs, dates, nuts and pomegranates.

The usual farm animals were donkeys, oxen, sheep and goats. Donkeys were used to transport people and things, and oxen to do heavy work. The sheep and goats were brought to pasture together, and it was usually the landowner's son who took care of them. Sheep were raised especially for their wool, which was used to make clothing, and goats were prized for their milk and meat.

seeing your companions in the faith being tortured."

Where are you buried?
"In the church of St. Bartholomew in Rome."

Tell me, was it worth it?
"What a 'pagan' question.... I learned to love God and my fellow human beings."

Matthew, the First Evangelist

*"As Jesus traveled...
he saw a man named
Matthew seated at a
tax booth, and he said
to him, 'Follow me!'
And he got up and
followed Jesus."*
(Matthew 9:9)

Are you called Matthew or Levi?

"I had two names, both of them Hebrew. It was common in Israel to have two names. For example, Mark, the evangelist, was called John Mark. Barnabas was also called Joseph...."

How did you become a disciple of Jesus?

"All he had to do was say, 'Follow me!' It happened on a day like any other while I was sitting at the tax table at the gates of the city. I was a tax collector in Capernaum, the center of commercial trade between the territory of Herod Antipas and that of his brother Philip. The merchandise traffic between Damascus in Syria and the Mediterranean coast passed right through Capernaum."

Did people respect you?

"The people, the poor people, couldn't like tax collectors, or publicans, as we were called. We were bureaucrats in the service of those in power. People considered us as public sinners, on a level with prostitutes. A proverb circulated about us. It stated: 'Every publican is a thief.'"

Were you respected by those in power?

"We were banished from the society of all honest people. It was considered improper to eat and drink with us. We weren't accepted as judges nor as witnesses at trials. The rabbis even considered us incapable of repentance and therefore already condemned. We were 'excommunicated *de facto*.' People were forbidden to accept charity from us publicans. It was considered permissible to trick and defraud us. Of course, people didn't have to be told that twice!"

Then why did Jesus stop and call you to be one of his faithful followers?

"When he looked at me, he definitely read my heart. I was in a deep spiritual crisis. I had already heard about Jesus of Nazareth. People said that perhaps he was the Messiah. I didn't want to believe it in a way, but on the other hand, I was looking for some hope that the system could be changed. I didn't enjoy seeing the poor people being ruined by taxes. I thought about it a lot. I hoped that our God would reveal a new way to us."

Jesus was criticized by the Pharisees for having dined in your house....

"But he silenced them by saying that he had come to call not the just but sinners. He was very kind to me—never looked down on me."

You are the only evangelist who uses the word "church." Why do you use it?

"The word 'church' is a translation of the Aramaic word 'qahal,' which means community. I tried to explain to the Christians and to people thinking of coming over to us from Judaism that a new community had been born."

In your Gospel you never call

Jesus the Son of God: you speak of him only as the Son of David. Why is that?

"I did that so my fellow Hebrews wouldn't get angry. They didn't like to say God's name or hear someone use it. Even when speaking of the kingdom of God, I used the expression 'kingdom of heaven.' But it's the same thing....

"Incidentally, although I'm willing to talk about my Gospel as if it's all my own work—it really isn't. I just did some early work that someone else built on years later. Mark's was the first Gospel to come out in what might be called 'final form.'"

I see. How many miracles did Jesus perform?

"How can anyone say?"

How many miracles are described in your Gospel?

"Are you a lover of statistics? Well—to speak as if I had worked on the final edition—I described twenty miracles in my Gospel. In the Gospel of Mark, eighteen miracles are mentioned, three of which I do not refer to. Luke describes nineteen and John only eight. John is the only one who tells about the miracle of the raising of Lazarus.

"Miracles suggest that God approves the person who works them, so they are important for that. Most of Jesus' miracles were done to help people, so they also showed God's love and compassion."

Did Jesus have a regular trial?

"In front of the Sanhedrin, definitely not. It was held at night without the presence of witnesses in defense. The accusing witnesses themselves did not agree with each other. At the end, the death sentence was given immediately. According to the procedure of the time, the sentence was supposed to be announced on the day after the trial."

The term "Sanhedrin" has come up before. Could you tell me something about the Sanhedrin?

"I think both Caiaphas and Joseph of Arimathea will have something to say, not to mention Nicodemus. They have first-hand knowledge. My comments might be inaccurate or not too kind."

Fine. Let's go on to ordinary life. Were there schools in Israel?

"They didn't exist, or at least not the kind you mean. Religion and history were taught through oral stories. The rabbis in the synagogues taught the history and law of Israel. Girls learned domestic work from their mothers, while boys learned a trade from their fathers. There was a proverb that said: "'Anybody who doesn't teach a useful trade to his son is raising a thief.'"

Did children and babies have toys?

"Yes. They really liked toys that made noise, like bells, rattles and whistles. Girls played with dolls and doll clothes. And like children all over the world, Hebrew children played 'grownup,' that is, they imitated adults. In the town squares and the streets, they enjoyed imitating weddings and funerals. Jesus mentioned this once."

And how did adults have fun?

"With checkers and dice."

You mean dice already existed?

"They were different from today's dice with six faces. There were disc-shaped dice with two faces, and pyramids with four faces called *teetotum*. Although the game of dice was very popular, it was disapproved of, and Hebrew law did not permit a gambler to testify in court."

THE PUBLICANS, HATED TAX COLLECTORS

As in other countries under Roman rule, the Romans used a very simple system to collect taxes from the Hebrews. Basing their calculations on the census, which indicated the number of people, the composition of each family and respective occupations and properties, the Romans established the sum of money that each person should pay. They assigned the task of collecting the money to representatives recruited from the local population. These men agreed to pay the sum due to the Romans, then concerned themselves with obtaining from their fellow citizens the payment of various taxes (on property, or purchases, on food products...).

The tax collectors, or publicans, were naturally disliked by the Hebrews, not only because people did not like to pay taxes, but also because the tax collectors worked for the Roman oppressors and were usually dishonest. They profited from their job by growing rich, because they made people pay much more than they actually needed to pay.

This situation was so widespread and common that for the Hebrews the word "publican" became a synonym for sinner. That is why Jesus caused surprise and alarm every time he associated with a tax collector. For example, this happened in Jericho when Jesus stayed with Zacchaeus, the head of the tax collectors. Zacchaeus welcomed him to his home with joy. He told Jesus that he was ready to restore whatever he had acquired unfairly. But the people criticized Jesus, saying "He went to stay in a sinner's house!"

Were there any other games?

"There were also balls like billiard balls. People would throw them to knock down objects, somewhat as you do in bowling today, but throwing the ball instead of rolling it. Outdoors they would throw leather balls. Everyone was good with a slingshot and stones. Another pastime which was quite popular was shooting at a target with a bow and arrow."

Would you give any advice to

the tax officials of today?

"Yes: 'Don't judge others, for with the judgment you judge, you will be judged.' Judged by God, naturally!"

What passage of the Gospel did you not write but would like to have written?

"The one about the adulterous woman found in John's Gospel, chapter 8, where Jesus says, 'Let whoever is without sin among you be the first to throw a stone at her.'"

Thomas, Patron of Doubters

"And a week later his disciples were once again inside, and Thomas was with them. Although the doors had been locked, Jesus came and stood in their midst and said, 'Peace be with you!' Then he said to Thomas, 'Bring your finger here and look at my hands, and bring your hand and put it in my side, and be not unbelieving but believing!' Thomas answered and said to him, 'My Lord and my God!' Jesus said to him, 'You've believed because you've seen me; Blessed are they who haven't seen yet have believed!'"
(John 20:26-29)

Blessed are they who haven't seen but have believed. Do you agree?
"How can I help it? These are words of the risen Jesus and may be considered the 'ninth beatitude.' But I know what

you mean: people consider me the patron of the doubting. There have always been 'doubting Thomases'—and there always will be—because doubt is part of human nature."

What happened exactly?
"I wasn't there when Jesus ap-

peared to the other apostles after the crucifixion, and I didn't believe in his resurrection. I raised problems and doubts, loudly and vehemently, in accord with my character."

And Jesus returned among the apostles and showed you

his wounds. How did he act toward you?

"He both comforted and reprimanded me: he convinced me but didn't condemn me. That's the nicest thing that can happen to a doubter if he or she wants to come out of the dark."

"Doubting Thomas" isn't the only expression in the New Testament that's become part of everyday language some place or other in the world. Could you explain some of these? For example, what about the expression, "acting like a Cyrenean"?

"That means to bear the burdens of others. It refers to Simon of Cyrene, who helped Jesus on the journey toward Golgotha. In Luke 23 we read: 'As they were leading him away they seized Simon of Cyrene, who was coming from the country, and laid the cross on him to carry behind Jesus.'"

And "to send from Herod to Pilate"?

"Pontius Pilate, who didn't want to judge Jesus, sent him to Herod Antipas. Herod sent him back to Pilate so he wouldn't have to take the responsibility. This expression is used when a citizen is bounced around from one office or window to another by public clerks who don't want to take

responsibility in helping the person with his or her problem."

May I go on? "He's as skinny as the horse of the Apocalypse"?

"They say that about someone who's all skin and bones. The Apocalypse is another name for the *Book of Revelation*, the last book of the Bible. In that book four riders appear. The first, on a white horse, is holding a bow in his hand (tyranny); the second, on a red horse, is holding a large sword (war); the third, on a black horse, has a scale in his hand (hunger); and the fourth, is

mounted on a deathly pale horse (death)."

To refer to someone who's badly injured and bleeding, they say "Ecce homo," or "Behold the man." Why is that?

"This saying refers to Jesus who had been whipped and was bleeding, and was wearing the crown of thorns on his head. John says in chapter 19 of his Gospel: 'Jesus came outside, wearing the crown of thorns and the purple robe. "Look at the man!" Pilate said to them.'"

What does "he's a white-washed tomb" mean?

"It's a term used for a hypocrite—you know, someone who pretends to be one way but really isn't. This phrase is taken from chapter 23 of the *Gospel of Matthew* where Jesus says, 'Woe to you, scribes and Pharisees, you hypocrites! You're like white-washed tombs, which outside appear beautiful, but inside are full of dead men's bones and all kinds of impurity. You too appear to be righteous on the outside, but inside you're filled with hypocrisy and lawlessness.'"

And "to go from Hosanna to the crucifixion"?

"To go from glory to misery. The saying is taken from the life of Jesus. He was welcomed with 'Hosannas' and applause at his entrance into Jerusalem—the event that you commemorate on Palm Sunday—and was then condemned to death soon afterward by the crowd who yelled, 'Crucify him!'"

What does the expression "to be a good Samaritan" mean?

"To have compassion for someone, to help those in danger or in difficulty, with unselfishness and concern for others. In Luke's Gospel, a story is told about a good Samaritan (a person from Samaria) who helps a man who was robbed and beaten by bandits. Before the Samaritan came along, other people had seen the injured man, but they hadn't helped him."

Among the inhabitants of Samaria (a region between Galilee and Judea), there's the saying, "Don't mix the Hebrews with the Samaritans." What does that mean?

"It means: 'Don't mix the holy with the unholy.' The Hebrews didn't want to be confused with the Samaritans. The Samaritans were of mixed ancestry and didn't completely follow the Mosaic law. The Jewish people of my time felt that the Samaritans were, in a sense, contaminated. That's what makes Jesus' story of the good Samaritan so striking. By showing selfless compassion, the Samaritan showed true holiness."

Thomas, where do you stand on the list of the apostles?

"The evangelists put me in the second group of four. In the first group are the brothers Simon Peter and Andrew and the brothers James and John. I'm always listed with the two great friends, Philip and Bartholomew, and with Matthew the publican. By the way, I was also called Didymus, which means 'twin.'"

Besides being the doubter, you were also one of the most generous members of the group.

"I guess that went along with my impulsiveness. But I didn't always follow through. In chapter 11 of John's Gospel, I'm correctly quoted as saying: 'Let's go, too, so we can die with him!' At that moment, I was ready to die with Jesus. But things were different on Good Friday...."

We're indebted to you for something you said at the Last Supper. You said to Jesus, 'Lord, we don't know where you are going! How can we know the way?' If you hadn't asked that question, we might never have had one of Jesus' most famous statements.

"You mean when Jesus said, 'I am the way and the truth and the life; no one comes to the Father except through me.' Yes, that really was a profound statement. I'm still reflecting on it."

Was it hard to be an apostle?

"I was an apostle because I was called to do it. God gave me the strength, but he didn't remove all the suffering. Yes, at times it was hard, but it was worth it."

Is it true that you went to India?

WHAT LANGUAGE DID JESUS SPEAK?

Jesus usually spoke Aramaic, the language used by the people of the holy land at that time. He also certainly knew how to speak Hebrew, since it was the scholarly language of Israel, the one in which almost all of the books of the Old Testament were written. In fact at the age of twelve Jesus was already able to discuss Sacred Scripture with the scholars at the temple. We know this from Luke's Gospel, chapter 2. Jesus also had to know some Latin and Greek—at least enough to understand and be understood.

Greek was the international language of the time (as English is today). Greek was the language used officially in all of the eastern parts of the Roman Empire, especially in commercial trade. It was also the spoken language of some of the places that Jesus visited, like Decapolis (east of the Jordan) and districts along the Mediterranean coast. On the other hand, Latin was the language of the Romans at the time when they occupied and governed the holy land. We may suppose that the speeches given by Pontius Pilate and other Romans were delivered in Latin.

The fact that Greek and Latin were familiar languages to the people of the holy land two thousand years ago, can be seen in chapter 19 of the *Gospel of John*, where we read that above Jesus' cross there was a sign saying: "Jesus of Nazareth, the King of the Jews." The words were written in three languages: Hebrew, Latin and Greek.

"Even though there are a lot of legends about me, I won't deny that I brought the Good News to India."

Is it true that you wrote a Gospel about Jesus' childhood?

"With those picturesque miracles that he performed in his father's carpentry shop? They're apocryphal writings. They're attributed to me because someone wanted to give them the authority of an apostle."

Why did the newsy and imaginative apocryphal writings become popular?

"They served to make known the places where Jesus lived and where the apostles carried out their mission. If you read them today, they describe in an interesting way certain forms of primitive Christianity that are of some historical importance. They also represent the beginning of a kind of Christian literature that was an alternative to pagan literature and was easily and widely distributed."

Could you tell me one or two of the legends that were started about you?

"Gladly. In one of them, it's told that when the apostles were reunited in Jerusalem, they drew lots to see where each one was supposed to go to preach. I had India, but I didn't want to go there. Then Jesus reappeared and convinced me to leave. He sold me to an Indian official in the service of a king who needed an expert in construction work."

Who was this king?

"His name was Gundafor. According to the legend, I distributed to the poor the treasures that were entrusted to me to build the royal palace. Because of this, I was imprisoned. But then I was immediately released because the king's brother, who had recently died, appeared to the ruler saying he had seen in heaven the palace built by Thomas."

In paintings you're portrayed with a belt. Why is that?

"It's the Sacred Belt which, according to another legend, was given to me by Mary, Jesus' mother, because I couldn't believe that she had been taken into heaven."

So even in legends you're a doubter?

"Yes, I'm afraid so."

James of Alpheus, Man of Mystery

"Now these are the names of the twelve apostles: first Simon who is called Peter and his brother Andrew, and James son of Zebedee and his brother John, Philip and Bartholomew, Thomas and Matthew the tax collector, James son of Alpheus and Thaddeus, Simon the Zealot and Judas Iscariot, who handed him over."

(Matthew 10:2-4)

James, who exactly are you?
"I know why you're asking that question. Not too many years ago, Catholics would have glibly stated that I'm an apostle, a relative of Jesus, the first bishop of Jerusalem and the author of the Letter, or Epistle, of James. But now scholars aren't so sure."

Then, you're not all of the above?
"I prefer to neither affirm or deny most of it and just let all the experts keep guessing. After all, it doesn't matter what my claim to fame was, as long as I tried to follow Jesus to the best of my ability. I do acknowledge that I'm James, son of Alpheus, one of the twelve apostles. As for the rest, I'm amused at scholars' attempts to figure it out...."

Most of the questions I've prepared are directed to "James, the brother of Lord." Although you don't admit to that title, would you be willing to respond to these questions?
"No problem."

Thank you. Then is "James the Just" the brother of Jesus, as the New Testament suggests?
"That story about Jesus' brothers has bothered people for centuries. But they forget that Mary was a Virgin and that in my culture we had no special word for 'cousins,' so we called most of our relatives simply 'brothers' and 'sisters.'"

So "James the Just" wasn't a brother of Jesus but some sort of cousin?
"That's correct."

Why wasn't Jesus well received by the people?
"Maybe because they were envious of the 'career' that he was making for himself. A rabbi with no formal training.... Some of them called him 'the carpenter'; others called him 'Mary's son.'"

What was so bad about that?
"We Hebrews hardly ever mentioned a son by his mother's name; if we did, it showed disrespect."

Now back to this "brother of the Lord"—was he the bishop of Jerusalem?
"Yes, but the word 'bishop' wasn't used yet. James the Just was head of the Christian community in the holy city for several years. The various apostles had gone to preach throughout the whole world as we knew it. This included Peter, the head of the group. Of course, sometimes one or more would return to confer about new developments...."

What was Jerusalem like in your day?
"Looking up from the valley of the Cedron brook, you could see Jerusalem on the hilltop above, dominated by the wonder of the completely new temple—in fact, in my day, they were still working on the final touches. Next to the ancient city, a new city of Hellenistic style had sprung up. Herod had that part built so that his capital would be as great as the other cities of the Roman Empire. The most strict Hebrews kept their distance from this pagan 'district.'"

What were the Roman soldiers like who occupied your country?
"Some were arrogant, but others had earned people's respect. It's true that a group of soldiers amused themselves torturing Jesus, but in general they were fair. Once, a Roman officer saved Paul from being lynched."

Is it true that James the Just was the most Jewish of the early Christians?
"It's true if you mean that James the Just is the New Testament figure best known for respecting the law of Moses and the rules of our people."

Who exactly were the Jewish Christians?
"After the descent of the Holy Spirit many Hebrews became followers of Jesus. (And, of course, we apostles were also Hebrews.) We all followed Jewish ways, for the most part, and added on obedience to Jesus' teachings, Christian

baptism and the celebration of the Eucharist. We started out as a Jewish sect. Soon, besides the Jewish or Judeo-Christians, there were also Gentile Christians—converts from pagan religions."

Let's assume for a moment that you—James of Alpheus—are also "James the Just," leader of the Jerusalem church, cousin of Jesus. What was your position regarding Judaism and Christianity?

"Going along with your assumption, I can say that as a Judeo-Christian I scrupulously observed the laws of Moses. I went to pray in the temple. I was well respected because, besides preaching the word of Jesus, I also preached the most scrupulous observance of the Mosaic law."

But wasn't that a contradiction?

"Absolutely not. I preached circumcision, respect for the day of rest, observance of prescribed foods.... But all this was part of our culture, our traditions."

Were the non-converted Hebrews your friends?

"They considered us a heretical sect. They called us the "minin," the heretics, and urged their faithful to cut off

THE HOLY CITY

Jerusalem, the principal city in the holy land, was and is the religious capital of the Hebrews, and the birthplace of Christianity. Jesus regularly went there for religious festivals. He was arrested, tried, and crucified there; there he died and rose. The apostles received the Spirit there, and went forth from Jerusalem to bring the Good News to the world.

The city dates back to around 3,000 B.C. It was a Jebusite stronghold when King David conquered it in 1,000 B.C. David constructed his royal palace in the city, which therefore began to be called the "City of David."

Jerusalem is often called "Zion," after one of the hills on which it is situated. With the transfer of the Ark of the Covenant by David and especially with the construction of the temple by Solomon, Jerusalem became the holy city which all Hebrews had to visit at least once in their lifetime.

At the time of Jesus, Jerusalem stood atop two hills about 2,725 feet above sea level. It had a population of about 100,000. This number often rose to 250,000 during religious feast days, especially Passover.

In addition to the splendid temple built by Herod, rich with white marble and gold-covered walls, the newer part of the city also had Greco-Roman buildings: the theater, the amphitheater, and the circus. The western part, situated on the highest hill, had a royal palace flanked by three tall towers. On the eastern hill, besides the temple, there was the Antonia fortress, a huge building that had porticoes and gardens, and was surrounded by a deep moat. Roman soldiers were stationed there.

all relations with us."

Could you tell me what you've written?

"People have attributed an apocryphal Gospel to me. This 'Gospel' tells that two elderly people, Joachim and Anne, the parents of Mary, brought her to the temple at the age of three to be raised there."

You also wrote a letter that's part of the New Testament—or am I mistaken?

"That's another point that scholars now debate. They think that toward the end of the first century someone wrote that letter under the name of James the Just. (James was martyred in A.D. 62.) I know that must sound strange to you, but writing under a famous person's name was a common enough practice in my day."

What's the message of the letter?

"That faith without written works is dead, useless. The letter urges people to bear suffering with patience and to be not only listeners but also doers of the word of God, to practice charity and observe the commandments, to restrain their tongue, to resist passion, not to desire worldly goods, not to oppress the poor...."

Did Jesus condemn wealth?

"Jesus didn't exclude the wealthy from his mission of salvation. He wasn't against the rich, but he was against any wealth that would poison people's hearts and make them unworthy of God and unjust toward their brothers."

At what age did a Hebrew boy become an adult?

"At thirteen, the *katù* (the little boy) became a *gadòl*, that is, an adult, a 'son of the law,' who from then on was treated as a man, no longer subject to the authority of his father."

Why was Jesus called "rabbì"?

"They called him 'rabbì,' or teacher, as an affectionate way of honoring his wisdom. The true rabbì had to follow regular higher studies, learning the art of reasoning from the scribes, the doctors of the law."

How many languages did Jesus know?

"He knew Hebrew perfectly, and Greek and Latin quite well, but when he spoke and preached he used Aramaic, the everyday language of the people of my country. Very few people would have understood Jesus if he had spoken in Hebrew. Toward the thirteenth century before Jesus, the Arameans were nomad tribes who settled down and created kingdoms in the "fertile crescent," that is, the territory contained in a great geographical curve (in the shape of a crescent-moon) which included Mesopotamia, Syria and Egypt. The Aramean kingdoms were soon overpowered by the great empires. But their language survived in Persia as well as in Egypt, Asia Minor, Afghanistan and also my homeland."

Why was the Sabbath day sacred for the Hebrews?

"Keeping the Sabbath was one of the laws of Moses that had been given on Mount Sinai. At the end of every week, Israel entered the Sabbath, as one enters a church for prayer. It was a day of rest and of worship. On Friday at nightfall, a trumpet was sounded from the highest roof in the town, two sounds, three times each. Those working in the fields stopped immediately; merchants closed up their stores; the craftsmen abandoned their workshops; and at home the women lit the sabbatical lamp, the symbol of celebration."

Did Jesus abolish this holy day?

"Not at all. In fact, Christians observed it up until the council of Nicea, which took place in 325. But Jesus did have a new approach to the Sabbath. He refused to make the Sabbath an unchangeable institution. For him, the Sabbath had been made for people and not vice versa."

And what does that mean?

"When rules become harmful or useless, they need to be changed. Jesus expressed this concept by citing David, who fed his hungry companions with the sacred bread reserved for the priests."

Which prayer do you like best?

"The one Jesus taught us and which is still recited today: 'Our Father who art in heaven....' "

Simon the Zealot, a Fighter for the Gospel

"It happened in those days that when Jesus went out to the mountain to pray he spent the night in prayer to God. When day came he called his disciples to him and he chose twelve of them, whom he also called apostles—Simon, whom he also named Peter, and Andrew his brother, and James and John and Philip and Bartholomew and Matthew and Thomas and James son of Alpheus and Simon, who was called the Zealot, and Judas son of James and Judas Iscariot, who became a traitor."
(Luke 6:12-16)

Why did they call you the Zealot?
"Most of the time, they called me 'the Canaanean' to distinguish me from Simon Peter. But it's true that even that name means someone who is zealous."

63

Who were the Zealots?

"They were 'freedom fighters,' the revolutionaries of the Jewish people, who tried to organize themselves to free my country from Roman rule. The Zealots were also opposed to the payment of taxes to Rome."

Were you a Zealot?

"I was a fervent patriot who was convinced that subjection to Rome was a betrayal of God, the true king of Israel. I was also full of zeal for God."

What was the holy land like in your day?

"My country was one of the regions most badly treated by the imperial misgovernment of Rome. It had become a part of the Roman Empire when General Pompey arrived in Jerusalem with his invincible army, a real war machine."

When did that happen?

"Before I was born. It was back in the year 63 B.C. The Jewish fighting men barricaded themselves in the temple and fought with the strength born of desperation, but they didn't want to give up the Sabbath rest that was imposed by their religion. So on the Sabbath they didn't fight. Pompey couldn't believe the unexpected opportunity."

THE ROMAN ARMY

I n New Testament times, the whole Mediterranean world lived substantially in peace under Roman rule. The emperor, Augustus, having concluded the period of conquest, was concerned mostly with establishing a just government and a correct administration of the provinces. The army was made up of twenty-five legions placed along the borders to defend the conquered territories against attack from the barbarian lands beyond and to discourage disorder and rebellion within the empire.

The holy land was restless under Roman rule, so the presence of Roman soldiers in the region was therefore normal. The Hebrews certainly did not love the Roman soldiers, for they were a sign of foreign domination. Besides, the soldiers showed little sympathy for the Hebrews, treating them like servants. But even among the military men there were some—especially centurions and other officers—who gained the respect of the people because of their uprightness, tolerance and sense of justice.

Only in cases of revolt and rebellion did the army intervene forcibly. And that was what happened in A.D. 66 when, because of the greed of the Roman procurator, the Hebrews tried to revolt. To restabilize the situation, Nero sent Vespasian with a large army. In A.D. 69 Vespasian became emperor and entrusted the continuation of the campaign to his son Titus. In the year 70 Titus wiped out Jerusalem, destroying its defenses and the temple.

And how did it end?

"12,000 people were massacred. Later, there were other revolts, too, but they all ended in blood baths. Thousands of my countrymen were sold as slaves until Augustus made Judea a kingdom subject to the Romans under the rule of an ally king, Herod I."

How many inhabitants did your country have at the time of Jesus?

"About two and a half million people lived there, one hundred thousand of whom were crowded into Jerusalem. There was no racial or religious unity. On the contrary, in some cities most of the inhabitants were Gentiles, that is, non-Hebrews, especially Greeks and Syrians. The countryside, on the other hand, was entirely Jewish, composed of strict, industrious, obedient farmers and small craftsmen. They spent their lives working, praying, fasting and waiting for the coming of the Messiah. They believed that the Messiah would establish his kingdom."

Were the Hebrews already good at business?

"They didn't do much business in my country at that time. There wasn't much opportunity to exercise the genius for which the Hebrews would later become famous."

Jesus foretold the fall of Jerusalem, which took place forty years after his death. You must have experienced those dramatic days firsthand. What happened?

"In A.D. 66 there was a revolt throughout the whole country and the numerically small Roman army had to evacuate the territory in a hurry. Our freedom didn't last long, though. In the year 69 the Roman legions arrived—60,000 men led by Vespasian, who took control of Galilee and Judea."

But wasn't it Titus who led the military campaign?

"When Vespasian was proclaimed emperor, the com-

65

mand of the troops went to his son Titus. They still had to conquer Jerusalem, where thousands of my countrymen had gathered."

And what did Titus do?

"At first he tried to conquer the city by surprise, but there were too many losses. So he decided on a tiring siege that lasted for many months. In May of 70, the Romans took over the first boundary wall of the city, and then the middle tower. My countrymen withdrew to the temple and to the Antonia fortress and kept up their desperate resistance.

"On July 24, a group of about twenty Roman soldiers got into the Antonia fortress and conquered it. The temple remained as the last pocket of resistance."

At that point, wouldn't it have been best to surrender?

"Titus tried to negotiate, but the leader of the resistance, John of Gischala, answered him with contempt. They resisted for another month, then the temple was set on fire, and a real massacre began in the streets of Jerusalem."

And what about the temple?

"It was completely destroyed. All that was left standing was a wall, the one that's called the 'wailing wall.'"

How many people died?

"A large number, but I don't know how many. Certainly not the two million that some historians say. The Roman historian Tacitus talks about 600,000 dying, but even that may be exaggerated. Some of the survivors who couldn't stand the defeat had themselves killed by the Roman soldiers; some committed suicide; some were made slaves and shipped to various other parts of the empire; others escaped and left the holy land. The dispersion of the Hebrew people, which had begun six centuries earlier—at the time of the exile—became almost total. It would be another 1,900 years before there would be a Jewish state again."

That's the State of Israel.

"Yes."

Is it true that Titus also brought a Jewish princess to Rome as war booty?

"I don't know. So many Hebrews entered Rome as slaves behind the triumphant chariot of the conqueror. The Romans celebrated wildly. They even dedicated an arch—they liked to build triumphal arches. But in that situation, there was no military valor on the Romans' part. They destroyed a poorly armed population in a desperate, impossible struggle."

Now tell me a little about yourself. Where did you carry out your apostolate?

"I preached mostly in Judea."

How were you treated?

"Quite well. At the beginning it was difficult, because I had a Galilean accent. I didn't get discouraged, though. As a young man, I had fought for the freedom of the Jewish people. Later I 'fought' for the Gospel, to bring everyone the message of salvation and love preached by Jesus."

According to tradition, you led the church of Jerusalem after James' death in 62. Is it true that you died a martyr at a very old age?

"To quote a biblical phrase, I died 'old and full of years.'"

Is there something that Jesus said that you'd like to share with us?

"This thought: 'I'm sending you off like sheep among wolves. Be wise....'"

Jude Thaddeus, Saint of the Impossible

"Then he went up on the mountain and called those he wanted, and they came to him. He chose twelve, whom he also called apostles. They were to stay with him so he could send them out to preach and to have power to drive out demons. He chose the Twelve and he gave the name Peter to Simon, and James son of Zebedee and James' brother John, and he gave them the name Boanerges, that is, Sons of Thunder, and Andrew and Philip and Bartholomew and Matthew and Thomas and James son of Alpheus and Thaddeus and Simon the Zealot and Judas Iscariot, who handed him over."
(Mark 3:13-19)

Doesn't it bother you to have the same name....

"As Judas the traitor? Why should it? He's Iscariot, and I'm Thaddeus, which means 'generous.'"

For many people, the name Judas has become synonymous with traitor....

"Yet before Iscariot made it hateful, Judas was one of the most beautiful names in the history of the people of Israel. One of Jacob's sons was named Judas (Judah), and one of the twelve tribes, the one that the Messiah would be born in, was named after him. Another Judas was considered a national hero. That was Judas Maccabeus, who led the Jewish revolt against Antiochus IV."

Were you a relative of Jesus?

"Some people think I'm one of the cousins of Jesus mentioned in the Gospels. I may have been, but I'll leave that for the 'experts' to figure out."

Where did you grow up?

"In farming country."

Do you know what number occurs most often in the Old Testament?

"In order to give you an exact answer, I would need the help of a computer. I think that the number which recurs most often is seven. In fact, it has well-defined symbolic meanings. Seven stands for fullness, completeness. In the proverbs it means 'everything.' The days of creation are seven, the Lord sees everything 'with seven eyes,' a 'complete' human life is seventy years...."

And what about the number seven in the New Testament?

"When someone speaks about the woman possessed by seven demons, who was Mary Magdalene, they mean that she was completely possessed. Peter asks what the limits of forgiveness are: 'Are seven times enough?' Jesus responds that forgiveness must be seventy times seven—therefore, complete and without limit. Jesus' genealogical tree, which we find at the beginning of the Gospels of Matthew and Luke, is based on the number seven."

WEIGHTS AND MEASURES

Among the Hebrews, especially at the time of the Old Testament, weights and measures were very approximate. Length, for example, would be measured by the length of a man's arm, or the stretch of a bow. Distance could be measured by a day's walk. The principal units of measure were the thumb or the finger, the palm of the hand, the span of the hand, the cubit (about eighteen inches), and the reed (about ten and a half feet). Long distances were calculated by stadia (each around 607 feet) or the Roman mile, a measurement equivalent to 1,000 steps (around 4,960 feet).

Cereal grains were weighed out in "homers," which was the "amount a donkey could carry," while an omer corresponded to the quantity of manna the Israelites collected every day in the desert. A homer consisted of 100 omers.

Precious materials were measured by weights, but these were not the same for everyone. It often happened that to deceive their customers, merchants would use two series of weights, one for buying and the other for selling.

By New Testament times, however, things were a bit more precise. The units of weight most used were the shekel, mina and talent. Their value changed through the years. There were fifty or sixty shekels in a mina and sixty minas in a talent.

First, Jesus chose twelve apostles, and then the group of seventy-two disciples was formed. Do these figures mean anything?

"The number twelve represents the twelve tribes of Israel—that is, all of the Hebrew people, to whom Jesus preached the Good News before anyone else. In ancient tradition, the number seventy-two indicated all the peoples on the earth. This shows willingness to address not only Israel, but all people."

Why were the disciples sent to preach two by two?

"There's a reason of an historical nature. According to the customs of the time, testimony was valid only if it was presented by at least two people."

Could you tell me about the council of church leaders that took place in Jerusalem in the year 49? How did it originate?

"Upsetting news had reached Jerusalem from Syrian Antioch, where Paul and Barnabas were. Many Gentiles, that is, people who weren't Hebrews, were converting to Christianity. However, they wouldn't subject themselves to the provisions of the Hebrew law—they didn't want to be circumcised. It was a very delicate, serious case.

Most of us were still faithful to the Law. We went to the temple, and we didn't want to break with the Hebrew people and tradition."

Is it true that violent arguments broke out in that situation?

"It's true that there were some lively, heated discussions, but not enough to create a complete division. There were two currents of thought on this problem. Was baptism enough to be welcomed into the Church or was it indispensable to be circumcised? One current claimed that pagans could enter the Church if they accepted faith in Christ and committed themselves to observing the ancient law of Moses, beginning with circumcision and observing all the rules on the purity of food, contacts with the pagan world, the Sabbath rest and the traditional Jewish rites. The other current claimed that a person entered the Church by virtue of baptism only."

And how was the controversy settled?

"People coming from paganism only had to observe a couple of Jewish practices, which did not include circumcision."

Did you write something on the subject, too, or am I mistaken?

"Well, there's a letter that bears my name, but the experts don't believe that I wrote it. I'll let them have the last word. It's one of the shortest among the 'Catholic letters' of the New Testament. It was written for the Christians of Asia Minor, to warn them about false doctrines."

That letter speaks of "clouds carried along by the wind, but bringing no rain...."

"And...'trees that bear no fruit even in the autumn...wild waves of the sea, with their shameful deeds showing up like foam.' That means the people who disrupt and corrupt everything, those who deny Jesus. The author reminded his readers that serious penalties were reserved for people like that, as happened to the Israelites in the desert, to the rebel angels, to Sodom and Gomorrah...."

Where did you go to preach?

"Many places. My name has been especially linked with Edessa, an important caravan center in Mesopotamia. Who knows where my mortal remains are buried? Maybe in Persia, which is present-day Iran."

What were the religious beliefs of the Greeks at the time of Jesus?

"There was a lot of confusion. No one has ever invented as many gods as the Greeks. The Greek poet Hesiod said that nobody in the world could remember all of them. Some of these gods had their main home on Olympus, a mountain in Greece. Others lived in caves, in rivers, in trees or at the bottom of the sea. Another Greek poet complained that no one knew where to stash a bushel of grain anymore, because every hole was occupied by a god."

And what about Rome?

"The Romans had practically taken the Greek gods in bulk and had given them new names. Zeus had become Jove, Hera had changed her name to Juno, Aphrodite had become Venus, and so on. Before following the hateful road of persecution, the Romans were very tolerant of different religions, whether they came from far away Britain or from the East."

Could you tell me which missionaries of the early centuries of Christianity you especially admire?

"The list would be very long. Here are some names: Dionysius, the apostle of Gaul; Augustine, the apostle of England; Boniface, who went to preach the Gospel in Germany; Adalbert, who evangelized Prussia; Anscar, the apostle of Scandinavia; Villibrord, the evangelist of the Low Countries; Cyril and Methodius the apostles of the Slavs; Francis Xavier...."

Why are people so devoted to you?

"Perhaps because so little is known about me and yet I am an apostle. I guess it's partly because someone started to pray through my intercession and got results. The word spread."

Judas Iscariot, the Traitor

"While he was still speaking, behold, Judas, one of the Twelve, came, and with him a large crowd with swords and clubs from the chief priests and elders of the people. Now the one handing him over had given them the sign and said, 'Whoever I kiss is the one; seize him!' And he came up to Jesus at once and said, 'Hail, Rabbi!' and kissed him."

(Matthew 26:47-49)

Judas Iscariot....
"I know what you're going to say: that I'm the man who betrayed the Son of God, the one who committed an unforgivable crime. I've been carrying the weight of that betrayal for twenty centuries. I know that my name is used to describe traitors, but I can assure you that there were extenuating circumstances."

So you can defend yourself?
"Definitely. I loved my people and my land. I couldn't stand the presence of the Romans anymore. In all of Judea, people were anxiously awaiting the coming of the Messiah, the one sent by God. Everyone was talking about him. We would finally be able to be a free people again. Jesus had arrived, the one who—like Gideon and Deborah and the charismatic Maccabee brothers—would break the chains of Israel's slavery."

What are you saying?
"The history of the Hebrew people had been full of oppression, revolts and liberation. Many peoples had subjected us, but with the help of God we were always able to regain our freedom. But in 63 B.C. the Romans had arrived with their invincible legions."

What are you trying to prove?
"I wanted a free Israel. I didn't want my people to be slaves anymore. I didn't want to see horses carrying Roman soldiers through the streets of the holy city of Jerusalem anymore."

Let's backtrack a bit. Where are you from?
"My name, Iscariot, suggests to many people that my native

town was Kerioth in Judea. That would make me the only known Judean among the apostles. It is believed that all the others were Galileans."

What was your childhood like?
"I was raised in the hope of being able to live in a free country. I dreamed of following the one sent by God, who would lead us in revolt. I also dreamed of organizing armies that would face the Roman legions in open battle. Day after

day I waited for freedom."

Why did you follow Jesus?
"I realized that he must be the Messiah. So I decided to dedicate body and soul to him, to travel with him on the journey that would bring us to the liberation of Israel and the subjection of all peoples to God."

So you became one of the twelve apostles, and in fact, the treasurer of the group. But then....
"Let me go on. I followed him,

I listened to his words, I saw him perform miracles. There was no doubt that he was the Messiah. But he never spoke about military plans, weapons or tactics to be studied. I couldn't understand where he was going...."

For example?
"He said that the most unfortunate people would be the first in the kingdom of God. The blind would see, the crippled would walk, the lepers would be cleansed, and even the dead would be raised to life. I wondered how we would be able to liberate Israel with an army of beggars."

So you were thinking about a revolution?
"I wasn't the only one. There were hundreds of people who were sharpening their swords in the mountains, preparing young men for battle, ready to come down to the battlefield as soon as Jesus sent a signal. But that signal never came."

Was that why you betrayed him?
"I knew that the priests of the Sanhedrin wanted to speak to him. Evidently, they also wanted to know Jesus' intentions and plans for the liberation of Israel from Roman rule."

CURRENCY IN THE HOLY LAND

In the early days of Israel, the Hebrews, like everyone else, bought and sold things in trade. Each person's riches were based on the quantity of his possessions, especially how many animals he owned. Job, for example, is described as one of the richest men of his time because he is said to have owned 7,000 sheep, 3,000 camels, 500 oxen and 500 mules.

Later, precious metals, especially gold and silver, became important. They were kept in bars or made into rings and bracelets. Only in the seventh century B.C. did people begin to use real coins.

At the time of Jesus, three types of coins were circulating in Palestine: the official coins of the Roman empire (which included the denarius, one-half aureus and aureus), the Greek coins (one-half drachma, didrachma, tetradrachma, and stater) and the Jewish coins (which included the lepton and shekel). Their value depended on how much they weighed and the value of the metal used to make them: gold, silver, copper, bronze, or brass.

Judas agreed to deliver Jesus over to the chief priests for thirty pieces of silver. These probably were Jewish shekels. A shekel was equal to one Greek tetradrachma, or about four Roman denari. Considering that one Roman denarius was equal to the daily salary of a worker, the amount agreed on with the priests was fairly substantial. It represented about four months' wages.

You don't want to admit that you betrayed Jesus?
"Why can't I make myself clear? Jesus spoke about a 'kingdom' and I wanted to know, as everyone else did, what kingdom that was. I didn't mind that people of authority, namely the priests, would lead Jesus into clearly

stating his plan for the new kingdom. That was why I collaborated with the priests."

You couldn't avoid that kiss and that embrace, which were gestures of friendship?
"First of all, at the time, I didn't think that Jesus would be tried by the priests and then killed. That kiss was meant to identify him and point him out to the temple guards."

But wasn't Jesus known by everyone?
"Jesus was popular among the simple and humble people, not among the temple guards, who had the task of leading him to the priests."

I wonder.... Tell me what happened then.
"After Jesus' arrest and sentence to death, I realized that I had made a terrible mistake. Jesus had meant one thing and I had understood something else. I tried to give back the thirty coins the priests had given to me, but they laughed in my face. I threw them away, since I didn't know what to do with them. I shouted to the priests that Jesus was innocent, but they wouldn't pay attention. I definitely hadn't done this for the money. Jesus' arrest could have been the spark for the rebellion, for the revolt

of all the people against the Roman eagle."

The price of the betrayal was thirty pieces of silver. How much money was that?
"With that amount, you could free a slave."

How did you die?
"There are two traditions about that. One is that I hung myself from a tree."

They say that you went crazy. Is that true?
"That's slander. It's difficult to clearly define the limit between wisdom and craziness. Thousands of legends have been created about me."

How do you think of yourself?
"As someone who has lost out in every sense. Can't I hope for someone to excuse me?"

You're in no position to ask for sympathy—don't you agree?
"My ex-companions, the apostles and the evangelists, point to me as the one who betrayed Jesus. Between the lines, though, they try to find some justification. Luke and John say that 'Satan entered Judas.' And that's true, I think. I got carried away and let Satan enter."

Do you have anything else to say?
"Yes—I was too ashamed to ask for mercy after what I had done. That was the biggest mistake of all."

Matthias, Judas' Replacement

"A few days later there was a meeting of the believers, about one hundred twenty in all, and Peter stood up to speak. 'My brothers,' he said,... 'someone must join us as a witness to the resurrection of the Lord Jesus. He must be one of the men who were in our group during the whole time that the Lord Jesus traveled about with us, beginning from the time John preached his message of baptism until the day Jesus was taken up from us to heaven.' So they proposed two men: Joseph, who was called Barsabbas (also known as Justus), and Matthias. Then they prayed, 'Lord, you know the thoughts of everyone, so show us which of these two you have chosen to serve as an apostle in the place of Judas, who left to go to the place where he belongs.' Then they drew lots to choose between the two men, and the one chosen was Matthias, who was added to the group of eleven apostles."

(Acts 1:15-16, 21-26)

How did you become one of the twelve?

"Jesus was raised up after he died on the cross. Then he left the apostles to spread his message. Judas the traitor was no longer a member of the group. So Peter took the initiative of completing the number of apostles. He required that the choice fall on someone who had accompanied the apostles 'during the whole time the Lord traveled about with us.' Two candidates were left, Joseph, who was called Barsabbas, and myself, Matthias. After a prayer to God we cast lots and my name came out."

What does the name Matthias mean?

"It's a shortened form of Mattathias, which means 'gift of Yahweh,' that is, 'gift of the Lord.'"

What had your life been like as a follower of Jesus?

"I was a member of the group of seventy-two disciples whom Jesus choose to help the apostles spread his message. Jesus gave us instructions for our mission. He sent us to preach two by two and told us, 'Don't carry a purse or a bag or sandals, and greet no one along the way....'"

Why weren't you supposed to greet anyone?

"In the East a greeting was something more than your 'hello' or 'good morning.' Especially between people who met each other in their travels, a greeting turned into a long conversation, which naturally took a lot of time."

How did you feel—representing Jesus like that?

"It was awesome. Jesus said, 'Whoever hears you, hears me, and whoever rejects you rejects me. And whoever rejects me, rejects the One who sent me.'"

Why are the names of the apostles and not the names of the first disciples mentioned in the Gospels?

"I didn't know, but our names are written in heaven. Jesus often reminded us of this."

How did you manage to eat if you didn't bring anything with you?

"We found what was necessary in hospitable homes."

What was the most common drink in the holy land?

"Milk was widely used, because the water wasn't always drinkable. The most common drink, however, was wine. The homes of the wealthy had cellars containing quality wine that came from all over the Mediterranean area. The wine was kept in narrow, pointed earthenware jugs that were easy to cover with earth or sand to keep the liquid cool."

Coming back to Jesus, did you see him as a revolutionary?

"If he was, he was such for everyone. Whatever problem a person was facing, Jesus had a word that was different. He did away with prejudices, mistaken evaluations and poisoned feelings. If you can call him a revolutionary it was definitely in the positive sense."

THE SPREAD OF COMMERCE

The holy land was located between various capitals of international trade. In fact, it was crossed by roads from Syria and Asia Minor (modern Turkey) to the north, and Egypt and Arabia to the south. Even the merchants who traveled overland from Mesopotamia passed to the north of the Syrian desert and then headed southwest toward Phoenicia, the holy land and Egypt. These merchants usually transported their goods by camel, traveling in caravans to help one another in case of need and especially to protect themselves from the attacks of robber bands.

This intense commercial traffic began to involve the Hebrews little by little. Earlier they had not been interested or involved in commerce, chiefly because they could get everything they needed for themselves and their families right in their own land.

At the time of the New Testament, though, living conditions had changed and commerce became much appreciated. In Jerusalem in particular, the presence of the temple favored the sale of animals for sacrifice and objects needed for worship. This type of market had "invaded" the temple, occupying the first courtyard (the Courtyard of the Gentiles). Jesus did not like this. The Gentiles had a right to pray in his Father's house. One day, in fact, Jesus made a whip out of cords and chased the vendors of oxen, sheep and doves out of the temple, together with the money-changers.

Was the name Jesus common in your country?

"Yes, it was. Some even claim that Barabbas was called Jesus, too."

Was Jesus a true Hebrew?

"Zealots, Essenes, Sadducees, Pharisees—there were so many ways of being Jewish, so many different attitudes, in life and in relationships with the Roman occupiers. In the midst of the conflicts in his environment, Jesus never identified himself with one group or the other. He was beyond that. "You asked me if he was a true Hebrew. Yes, he was a true son of Israel."

The Zealots were men who wanted the liberation of the holy land. Who were the Essenes?
"They were a group that had withdrawn to the banks of the Dead Sea—at least, that's where a number of them lived. They had a community there and did manual labor. They also prayed and studied sacred books. They were hostile to the priestly world of Jerusalem, where people were largely concerned about power, wealth and comfort."

Did Jesus take a position against the movements in your country?
"He sure did! When he said, 'All who take up the sword will die by the sword,' he was speaking against the Zealots and other fanatic supporters of direct, armed action. Jesus also urged us not to follow the examples of the Pharisees and Sadducees. However, this didn't prevent him from having personal encounters with representatives of the various groups. He ate at the table of the Pharisee Simon and conversed with Nicodemus, who was from the leading religious body, the Sanhedrin. He visited the rich and the poor, he healed lepers, he made a disciple of a Samaritan woman and cured the daughter of a Syro-Phoenician woman. In short, he was very open toward everyone."

What do historians say about Jesus?
"Roman historians have ignored him and Jewish historians have said very little. Some Rabbinic documents say he was executed on the eve of Passover for having led the people astray."

Tell me about the other apostles. What were they like?
"They were like everyone else, with their good qualities and shortcomings. Judas, the one who betrayed Jesus, was the group's treasurer. Some people maliciously said that he was a little dishonest in managing the funds. Matthew, the ex-tax collector, was a good judge of people. Thomas was sometimes impulsive and sometimes hesitant. Peter was good-natured and simple, but every so often he had outbursts of anger. He was very kind to me. James was usually with his brother John, who was considered the intellectual of the group. Philip and Bartholo-mew were also usually together...."

Many writings have come out under your name, including the secret conversations of Jesus and Mary, the traditions of Matthias....
"And also a Gospel of Matthias. They're part of that enormous mass of literature that were hand copied and sent all over the world in the first years of Christianity. The Gelasian Decree took care of putting this material in order."

What was that?
"It was a decree that took its name from Gelasius, a pope who lived at the end of the fifth century. After thorough studies, this confusing material was organized. All the books of Christian origin were divided into two categories: those called 'canonical,' whose authenticity is not in question, for the Church holds that they're inspired by God; and the apocrypha, which are not the 'word of God.' But let's make it clear that the apocrypha have some interesting content, even though it's been romanticized in a rather imaginative way."

Where did you go to preach?
"If you're into legends, they sent me to Ethiopia and it was there that I died."

Mark, One of the First Christian Reporters

"Barnabas and Saul finished their mission and returned from Jerusalem, taking John Mark with them."
(Acts 12:25)

It's written in your Gospel that a young man covered with a sheet followed Jesus after his arrest. Was that you?
"That young man who was following Jesus and whom the guards were trying to get, wanted to carry out an act of desperate solidarity so that Jesus wouldn't be left alone. All the others had fled. There was so much sadness that night!"

So, you knew Jesus?
"Yes, at the end of his life. I was young, and Peter came often to my house and spoke to me about Jesus. I later gathered information from Peter and the other disciples to write my Gospel."

Scholars say that among the four evangelists, you're the best "reporter" in the modern sense. Do you agree?

"I tried to hand on the first message preached by Jesus, contained in this phrase: 'The Kingdom of God has come; repent and believe in the good news.' I tried to report many concrete details without too many comments. I wanted to make the feelings of the Lord—who presented himself to everyone as a man even though he was the Son of God—shine through his actions. And in telling about what Jesus said, I preferred a form of give-and-take dialogue with his audience. Don't ordinary people talk like that?"

Mark, could you explain to me the meaning of the transfiguration?
"That was a means for strengthening the faith of the three disciples who would be the most direct witnesses of Jesus' agony. In the transfiguration, Jesus changed his outward appearance, which was simply human, and let his own divine glory shine out. I questioned Peter many times about that event. Peter resorted to making comparisons because it was difficult to adequately describe a vision that was above our human level of understanding. I used a comparison, too. I wrote that Jesus' clothes 'became an utterly glistening white, so white that no

one on earth could bleach them that way.'"

You tell that during the multiplication of the bread the people were sitting "on the green grass," in "groups of a hundred and of fifty." How could you be so exact?

"I wrote with precision, but not in time order, everything that I could remember about the words and actions of the Lord. It was Peter who had told me about those things. I stayed by the apostle's side for many years, even in Rome. He affectionately called me 'my son.'"

In your Gospel, the Person of Jesus is emphasized more than his teaching. Why is that?

"I wrote the Gospel to make Jesus known to the Gentiles who had converted to Christianity. So I preferred to tell what Jesus did. That is, I tried to deal with the issues that were most suitable for readers who lived outside the holy land and knew little or nothing about Judaism."

What does the word "Gospel" mean?

"Your English word 'Gospel' corresponds to the Greek word for good news or happy announcement. In the biblical language of the Old Testament, that Greek word meant especially the 'announcement of victory.' So the Gospel is 'good news' indeed."

In what language were the Gospels written?

"They were written in Greek, which was the international language then. All, that is, except Matthew's earliest version. Matthew preferred to write in Aramaic, his mother tongue and the language that was spoken in Israel."

How long is your Gospel?

"It's the shortest one of the four. It consists of 661 verses. The longest one is by Luke, which contains 1,150 verses. In the *Gospel of Matthew* there are 1,068 verses; in John's there are 879."

Why was Jesus so successful?

"He preached things that were new with personal authority, unlike the scribes and doctors of law. They continually referred to the authority of their teachers."

What did Peter especially remember about Jesus?

"Well, one thing was his prayer. Every morning Jesus would rise early and go off to a solitary place to pray. Sometimes he would even pray all night."

What qualities are required to be a disciple of Jesus?

"Faith, love for one's neighbor and an effort to live a life pleasing to God."

Your Gospel is known for the famous "messianic secret."

What does that mean?

"Jesus would often tell his followers and persons cured by miracles not to reveal who he was. He knew very well that the Hebrews of his time were waiting for a Messiah who would free them from Roman rule and make them a powerful people. He constantly tried to emphasize that his kingdom was not of this world, that the freedom he announced was not political, but of the spirit, that his message was one of love and not violence. Therefore, because he feared that spreading the news about his preaching and his miracles could cause an armed revolt, he told the apostles over and over, at least in the early stages of his preaching, not to reveal that he was the Messiah."

Because of you, the two great apostles and friends Paul and Barnabas had an argument and separated. How did that happen?

"During the first missionary journey of Paul and Barnabas, I had been taken along against the judgment of Paul, who considered me too young for such a difficult journey. And, in fact, I left the mission in the city of Perga in Pamphylia, after traveling with them through Cyprus. I couldn't do it. It was too tiring for me and I returned to Jerusalem. Paul had been right, but Barnabas—my cousin—became stubborn and wanted Paul to bring me with them on the second journey also. Paul refused, and they separated. Afterward, though, everything got straightened out. Paul and Barnabas were reconciled. Later, I became a disciple of both Peter and Paul."

What did you do after the death of Peter and Paul?
"I left Rome and went to preach in Egypt, settling in Alexandria."

What was that city like?
"It was one of the most important cities of that time. A wide bridge that was almost a mile long connected the city with the island of Faros. Inside the great port was a dock which contained the royal galleys. Water from the Nile was channeled to numerous marble and granite fountains. In the center of the city were majestic monuments: the stadium, the amphitheater and the museum, with the famous library that would one day have a treasure of 700,000 volumes."

Where are you buried?
"Tradition has it that in 828 my body was transported by merchants from Alexandria to

WHAT LANGUAGE WAS THE NEW TESTAMENT WRITTEN IN?

While almost all the books in the Old Testament were written in Hebrew, almost all those in the New Testament were written in Greek. The first draft of the *Gospel of Matthew* was probably written in Aramaic, since Matthew wrote for the Hebrews to show them that Jesus was the Messiah they had been waiting for. The original draft, however, no longer exists, and the final version—greatly developed—was written in Greek, probably by someone other than Matthew.

In the old days, books had to be copied by hand so they could be circulated. Usually the copyists worked in groups under a head copyist; each one of them prepared a copy of the same book. This system helps to explain how easy it was/is to find more or less minor discrepancies between the texts. If one of the copyists heard a word incorrectly or was distracted for an instant, an error would occur.

But even a copyist working alone, reading the text to himself, could be distracted and make an error or could mistake a word that was not very clear.

In any case, biblical scholars possess thousands of Greek manuscripts of the New Testament, to which they can refer. By studying and comparing all those documents, to which are added the most ancient translations in Latin and other languages, scholars have provided us with texts of the New Testament which give the maximum guarantee of faithfulness to the original.

Venice. Since then, I've become the patron saint of that city, which built a magnificent basilica in my name."

Could you recite a phrase from your Gospel?

"'Whoever receives a child in my name receives me; and whoever receives me, receives not me but the One who sent me.' These are words of Jesus."

Luke, a Careful Historian

"Do your best to come to me soon. Demas fell in love with this present world and has deserted me, going off to Thessalonica. Crescens went to Galatia, and Titus to Dalmatia. Only Luke is with me."
(2 Timothy 4:9-11)

Are you Jewish?
"Scholars used to think I was a converted Gentile, but now they're not so sure. Yes, I could be Jewish. I'll keep everyone guessing."

Did you ever speak directly to Jesus?
"I never met him in person, but knew him through his apostles and disciples. My family lived in Antioch in Syria."

How did you manage to write the Gospel?
"I collected the testimony of those who had lived with Jesus

and obtained documentary evidence about some of the historical events of the time. I also had access to the early Christian Scriptures that were already being read in the assemblies when we gathered together to pray. I felt impelled to write because of the requests of the many converts who wanted an orderly text about the life and words of Jesus."

You were an educated man: a doctor it seems, and a writer and—according to legend—also a painter. How did you feel among Christ's disciples, who were uneducated?

"Paul, with whom I traveled at times, was a cultured man of extraordinary talent. Matthew knew a lot about the history of his people. Yet, although it may seem strange, education didn't matter much. All the apostles spoke a particular language and said things unknown to the wise men of the world. They spoke of love, forgiveness, salvation and equality; they said that God died for us. In becoming a Christian I had many things to learn. I didn't feel superior."

Did you really paint the first portrait of Jesus' mother, Mary?

"I painted the most beautiful portrait in my Gospel, which describes the events surrounding Jesus' birth."

Jesus is found everywhere in the Gospel. Why isn't Mary mentioned much?

"Mary is a key figure, but Jesus is the Son of God. In my Gospel we find Mary present before Jesus is born and present until after his crucifixion. She wasn't much more than a girl when she said 'yes' to the angel's disturbing request. But Mary was the first to understand that her child would not belong only to her. She wouldn't have wanted a larger place in the Gospel."

Could you describe your city, Antioch, to me?

"It was the third largest city of the Mediterranean world. It ranked after Rome and Alexandria. It had 500,000 inhabitants and two and a half miles of paved streets that were flanked by porticos, lots of fountains, indoor and outdoor markets, theaters, racecourses, and hot and cold bath houses. The Christians who had fled from Jerusalem during the first persecution in Judea took refuge in Antioch. It was in Antioch that Jesus' followers were called 'Christians' for the first time. After the year 40, it became the center of the Church's missionary effort, which it remained for a few years. The apostles Paul and Peter both preached and taught there."

After your wrote the Gospel, why did you write the Acts of the Apostles?

"To tell about the beginnings of the Christian community. I thought that the history of Jesus without the history of the Church would be incomplete. They consider me the first Christian historian, raised in the 'apostolic school' of Paul."

Let's talk about Paul for a moment. He said that women were to keep silent in the assembly—that they weren't allowed to talk at church gatherings. Was he an "anti-feminist"?

"That statement and others, often quoted out of context, have created the image of Paul as an anti-feminist, but it's not true. He was a great supporter of women's rights. We have to remember that before Jesus and Paul, women were treated like slaves or at least like children. In the letter to the Romans, Paul spoke with affectionate sympathy of women who had worked for the Lord. He called them 'sisters' and 'deaconesses of the Church,' emphasizing that they carried out a specific ministry of apostolate and charity. Paul taught that men and women have the same dignity, equal rights and equal duties. I'll read you one of his sentences on marriage: 'Husbands love your wives just as Christ loved the church and gave his life for it....' Do you think that someone who talks like that is an anti-feminist?"

Why did women have to keep quiet in the assemblies?

"It was a rule of behavior in the Jewish and Gentile world of that time. For one thing, women generally had little education then. Because of this, there would have been too many questions requiring explanations and clarification, which would have hindered the regular procedure of the sacred assemblies. Paul said that if women wanted to learn something, they could ask their husbands at home. And another thing—although Paul appreciated women's contributions to the Church, he didn't want to try changing the customs of society overnight."

Were you with Paul very much?

"I went with him on some of his trips and I was near him during his last imprisonment before his martyrdom."

Paul calls you, "our dear doctor." Was the medical profession common in those times?

"Yes. In Judea and Galilee, for example, every city had a doctor and even a surgeon. The woman who was suffering from a hemorrhage and who approached Jesus had been to many doctors. There was always a doctor present among the officials of the temple, too. He was responsible for curing the priests, who worked barefoot and easily caught certain diseases."

What were the Jewish opinions about diseases?

"In early times an illness could be considered a punishment inflicted on a sinner or it could be a test for a righteous person. According to certain traditions, calluses on the feet were considered a sign of the passing of an evil spirit. Polyps in the throat or nose were considered a punishment for serious sins, and so on."

So sick persons were avoided?

"Sometimes. Jewish law prescribed rigorous preventive measures against some illnesses. For example, it established rules for protection against contracting leprosy. Lepers had to leave their heads uncovered, wear special clothing, and, as a rule, live apart from inhabited areas. When they came near a town or city, they had to announce their presence by shouting, 'Unclean! Unclean!' This prevented spreading the disease by contact."

Were any efforts made to cure people?

"By New Testament times, yes. Two centuries before Christ, Ben Sira already spoke about doctors as instruments of God for people's health, so the mentality had changed a lot. In Jesus' time, the Essenes, the

ILLNESSES AND DOCTORS

What were the most common illnesses in Jesus' homeland? The most terrible one was probably leprosy, but typhus, cholera, dysentery, epilepsy, paralysis and dropsy were also well known. Disabled people—including the blind, the deaf, deaf-mutes and the crippled—were also common.

Blindness was caused chiefly by dust carried on the wind. Epilepsy, on the other hand, was attributed to the harmful effects of the moon, or to evil spirits that were believed to penetrate into the sick person.

In the Old Testament, not much importance was given to the cure of illnesses. Both good and bad came from God. Good health was considered a divine blessing, while illness was thought to be the consequence of a transgression, a sin. Only God could heal. Therefore, there wasn't much room for medicine, and even less for any surgical operations.

But, things began to change little by little. By the second century B.C., doctors had acquired importance and prestige. In Jesus' time, every city in the holy land had to have a doctor and perhaps even a surgeon. The rabbis recommended it. The medical profession, therefore, had become one of competence and respect.

Even Luke, Paul's collaborator and the author of a Gospel and the Acts of the Apostles, seems to have been a doctor. Since he knew Greek well, he probably could make use of the great medical tradition of the Greeks. That tradition had begun four or five centuries earlier, when Hippocrates of Cos had set forth the bases of medical science. Hippocrates handed down his teachings in sixty-three treatises and also established some principles of behavior for doctors. These principles included the one that the life and health of the patient must be the doctor's main concern—a principle still valid today.

group of 'monks' who lived near the Dead Sea, diligently studied the curative properties of plants and minerals."

What kinds of remedies were used in your time?

"Dates were prescribed for jaundice, olive oil with garlic for destroying intestinal worms, and parietaria roots for toothaches. For heart palpitations, barley soaked in curdled milk was used. Rheumatism was cured with mashed fish brine applied to the ailing parts. Honey was spread on wounds and sores, and the juice from the poppy flower was used as an analgesic."

Who helped a woman when she gave birth?

"There were midwives. Obstetrics was the only public profession of any prestige that was accessible to women. Since the beginning of the history of Israel, the midwives had formed a kind of corporation. They were usually very capable."

Did Jesus speak of illness as a punishment for sins?

"Definitely not. Once he said of a blind man, 'Neither he nor his parents sinned.' Therefore, Jesus would have felt it was up to medicine to study the causes

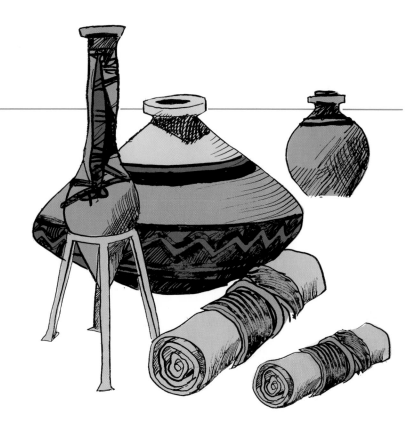

of illnesses and, if possible, to cure them."

Would you quote a phrase from your Gospel?

"'Don't judge, and you won't be judged. Don't condemn and you won't be condemned. Forgive, and you will be forgiven, give, and it will be given to you.... For with the measure you measure, it will be measured out to you in return.'"

Where can I read that?

"In chapter 6, verses 37 and 38."

Mary Magdalene, Missionary of Jesus' Resurrection

"Now when he rose in the early morning of the first day after the Sabbath he appeared first to Mary Magdalene, from whom he had driven out seven demons. She went to announce it to those who had been with him, who were mourning and weeping."

(Mark 16:9-10)

There are so many Marys in the story of Jesus! Could you explain the reason for this?

"I can only say that Miriam—Mary—was a very common name in Israel. Jesus' mother's name was Mary, and Mary was also the name of the sister of Lazarus and Martha, great friends of Jesus who lived in Bethany, a small town near Jerusalem. There was Mary of Clopas, who stood with us beneath the cross. And there was also me, Mary Magdalene, so called because I was from Magdala, a village a few miles from Tiberias in Galilee."

Are you the sinner?

"I was definitely a sinner, but not in the way many people think and not as artists and writers have depicted me for hundreds of years. I was not that woman who entered the house of Simon the Pharisee, approached Jesus and bathed his feet with her tears."

What was that woman's name?

"I don't know. She was known as the 'sinner of the city.'"

Did you love Jesus?

"I loved him just as the other Marys loved him. Jesus had cured me of a very serious illness by chasing away evil spirits. They said that there were seven of them. That could be. Great confusion resulted from this story. It started the legends that were repeated in literature and art about Mary Magdalene's conversion from a life of sin."

Yes, many painters have portrayed you as the sinner of the city. Does it bother you?

"I have no objections. Those are artistic interpretations. That sinner, who was full of devotion, courtesy and repentance, wasn't sent away. On the contrary, Jesus put his trust in her, forgave her sins and rehabilitated her in front of everyone, admitting her once again into ordinary human society. It was as great a miracle as any that healed the sick."

How did Jesus treat women?

"While the Hebrew culture—and most others, too—had placed women in silent subjection and submission, Jesus did and said things that represented an authentic revolution. He rejected the behavior common at that time. In telling parables, he referred with kindness to women and their world. He didn't think that a woman's intellectual ability was to be concentrated only on domestic chores. In daily prayer, the Jewish man thanked God for not being born a non-believer, a woman or a slave. Jesus turned this kind of attitude around. He had the utmost respect for women. He welcomed them, helped them, educated them, praised them, admired them and suggested them as models for how to act."

Tell me briefly about that day on Calvary.

"What a shameful scene! There was so much confusion! So much sadness! Mary, Jesus' mother, was standing with John. We other women were off to the side a bit, crying. Jesus had been nailed to the cross and the blood was dripping from his wounds to the ground, while people were laughing scornfully. The soldiers sat on the ground playing with dice. The centurion was the only serious person except for us. He was worried that the situation would get worse. Then everything was over. It was three o'clock in the afternoon, but it already seemed like night. Clouds blacker than any I had ever seen before thickened in the sky and a cold wind swept the hillside...."

Did you think that Jesus would rise?

"Not even the disciples who had always been close to him understood, so how could I have believed it? His mother understood something, I think, but how much? We had seen him die on the cross. We had seen a Roman soldier cruelly pierce his body with a lance. That thrust had opened another wound in his side."

And then what happened?
"A well-dressed man arrived running, followed by a lot of servants, who took Jesus' body down from the cross and carried it away. We women followed them to see where Jesus would be buried. We couldn't do anything because these were the last moments of the preparation day."

What did that it mean?
"The Passover was about to begin. All our feast days began with the evening twilight, you know—when three stars became visible in the sky. Before twilight everything necessary for Passover had to be prepared, for on that day all work was forbidden. We spent a very sad Passover waiting for the sun to set so we could go to buy the aromatic herbs to be used to embalm Jesus' body. In fact, on the following day—Sunday—the sun still hadn't appeared on the horizon when we hurried toward the burial place! Our greatest worry was how to move the heavy stone from in front of the tomb. Who would have so much strength?"

And then what happened?
"The tomb was empty! I became afraid that someone had stolen the body. I ran to tell the apostles, since I knew where they were hiding. Peter hesitated, then ran toward the tomb with John. By the time I got there, they were coming out again, shaking their heads. They walked away...."

What did you do then?
"I burst into tears. I couldn't stand the idea that nothing remained of Jesus, not even his body. When I turned around, I saw a man that I didn't know. I thought it was the man who tended the garden...."

But couldn't you tell that it was the risen Jesus?
"I didn't recognize him. It was impossible to recognize him, but I can't explain why. Only when he softly said my name, 'Mary,' did I recognize him! I fell at his feet. I was so happy...."

What did Jesus say to you?
"'Go to my brothers and tell them....' I ran again—as fast as I could—to tell them this good news! With my heart in my throat, I announced that Jesus had risen. But they didn't seem to believe me. 'Words of a woman,' I heard someone comment—that is, words that were less important than words uttered by a baby. They couldn't accept that Jesus, the Messiah, the man sent by God to change the world, had chosen a woman to announce that he had risen."

That is an interesting question. Do you know why you were the one whom Jesus appeared to for the first time, the one chosen as the "apostle" of the resurrection?
"I've never asked myself a question like that."

How did you judge those men who didn't believe you?
"I didn't blame them. In our mentality, it was unthinkable for women to judge men. We were only supposed to keep quiet."

Could you tell me about Mary and Martha, the sisters of Lazarus?
"Those two women were so different from each other! One was a great dreamer and romantic, while the other was practical and always making sure that there was never anything missing at home. Both were great women!"

What women of the twentieth century do you most admire?
"There are so many of them, but I want to mention at least two in particular: Edith Stein, the nun of Jewish origin who died with her people in a Nazi concentration camp, and Teresa of Calcutta, who has done so much for the poorest and most destitute people."

JEWISH FEASTS

One of the important feast days of the people of Israel was the Sabbath. Following the example of the Creator who, according to the Book of Genesis, rested on the seventh day, the Jewish people, too, observed a day of rest after six days of work. This day was dedicated to God. At a certain point, the Sabbath observance had become so strict and complicated that Jesus was forced to remind people that "the Sabbath was made for man, not man for the Sabbath." He was criticized time and again by the Pharisees for performing miracles on that day.

The Hebrews had many annual feasts. An important one was Passover, which was celebrated in the spring, in the month of Nisan. It commemorated the liberation of the Israelites from slavery in Egypt. At the Passover dinner and for the entire following week, the people ate unleavened bread—that is, bread made in a hurry, without yeast, in memory of the hurried preparations made by their ancestors before leaving Egypt. The week of the Unleavened Bread also had another meaning. It marked the beginning of the barley harvest, and the unleavened bread symbolized a new beginning. At the end of the week, the first sheaf of the harvest was presented to God.

Later, at the end of the wheat harvest, the Feast of Weeks was celebrated, which was also called by the Greek word Pentecost ("fiftieth") because it fell fifty days after Passover. This was also originally a harvest feast, but by Jesus' time it had acquired a second meaning—a commemoration of the covenant made at Sinai between God and the Israelites a few weeks after their departure from Egypt.

At the beginning of autumn, on the first day of the seventh month, there was the Feast of the Trumpets, which became New Year's Day, even though the months continued to be counted from Nisan. This autumn new year celebration may have its origin in a lost calendar followed before the exile.

On the tenth day of the seventh month, there was the day of Atonement (Yom Kuppùr) when the people asked God for forgiveness for their sins. It was the only day on which the High Priest entered the "holy of holies," the innermost and most sacred part of the temple. A few days later, the Feast of Tents or Booths (literally, huts) was celebrated. It was the third harvest feast, and it lasted one week. This was the happiest and most popular holiday of the year, during which the people lived in huts in the fields or even on the roofs of houses. Such huts were common in the fields, where they protected people from the heat. They easily became part of the great final harvest feast. By Jesus' time, this feast also commemorated the long period that Israel had spent in tents in the desert.

In the early winter, the Feast of the Dedication was celebrated. It commemorated the new dedication of the temple made by Judas Maccabeus after the violation of the temple by the king of Syria, Antiochus IV Epiphanes. This feast, also called Hanukkah, lasted a week and was quite similar to the Feast of Tents. It was also called the "Feast of Lights."

Finally, in the last month of the year, toward the end of winter, there was the Feast of Purìm, which lasted for two days. It dated back to the time of the Persian Empire and was the least religious of the Jewish feasts—a time for fun and gifts.

Martha, the Sister of Lazarus and Mary

"Now in their journeying he came to a certain village where a woman named Martha received him. She had a sister named Mary who seated herself at the Lord's feet and listened to his teaching. But Martha was distracted with all the serving, so she came up and said, 'Lord, doesn't it matter to you that my sister left me to serve alone?' In answer the Lord said to her, 'Martha, Martha! You're anxious and upset over many things, but one thing is necessary. Mary has chosen the better part, which will not be taken from her.'"
(Luke 10:38-42)

"Be like Martha and Magdalene" is a pleasant way of saying, "Keep busy, do a little of everything." What do you think about this?

"Well, I'm the patroness of housewives. Painters portray me with a bunch of keys in my hand or with kitchen utensils. I barely knew Magdalene, the woman who followed Jesus everywhere. I may have seen her a couple of times, but I never spoke with her."

Why did you run to the fire-place whenever Jesus came to your house?

"I didn't want him to lack any-thing. I ran to light the fire and prepare the young goat for roasting. There were so many things to do."

Would you tell me about your sister Mary?

"She was a great dreamer, a sweet woman who loved people. She was younger than I, but her concern for Jesus was like mine. Jesus was like a brother to us. Every time he left, especially if he was going to Jerusalem, my heart ached. I somehow knew that one day I would never see him again. I wouldn't be able to set a dish of soup in front of him any-more."

John the evangelist tells us that when Jesus went to Bethany a few days before his death and was a guest at Lazarus' house, "Mary took a pound of authentic lavender perfume, which was very precious, anointed Jesus' feet, and dried them with her hair." Evidently, Mary of Bethany must have had very long hair. All women, however, had long hair, even though they usually kept it out of their way by braiding it or piling it on top of their heads.

On the other hand, although Jewish men wore beards and long hair in ancient times, by the time of the New Testament they had begun to shave their beards and cut their hair. They were influenced by the styles of the Greeks and Romans.

Clothing, however, didn't change much in the course of the centuries. As a basic garment, the Hebrews wore a wide band around their hips or a type of short skirt that came down to their knees. Over that they wore a tunic made of wool or linen. A man's tunic was red, yellow, black or striped, and it reached down to the calf. For women, it was usually blue and came down to the ankle. Over the tunic, wealthy people wore elegant, light outer garments, often made of silk. For protection from the cold, a rich person would use a large cloak. For poor people and shepherds, the cloak was a dark color and made of coarse goatskin. It was very important because it also served as a blanket during the night.

The kind of shoes that we use today didn't exist. Poor people usually went around barefoot. The normal footwear for someone who was better off was a pair of sandals, made simply from a piece of hide the size of the sole of the foot with a long strip of soft leather which passed between the big toe and the second toe and was tied around the ankle.

Were you the lady of the house?

"Our parents weren't with us anymore, and I was the one who had to take care of the house. There was no conflict between Mary and me, if that's what you want to know. I considered her more a daughter than a sister. She needed protection and tenderness. She confided her worries and fears to me."

Did she help you around the house?

"Of course, and she was obedient, too. But she liked to spend time outside gazing toward Jerusalem or admiring the fields covered with red anemones or the olive trees that were crowded on the sides of the hill."

Where did you live?

"In Bethany, a flourishing village close to the holy city

When did you begin working?

"I've always known how to do housework and work in the fields. There are no dolls in my memories. If I think about my childhood, I see myself with my mother in front of the fire or walking with my father while he was sowing seeds. There were times when I too would have liked to have someone to turn to, to open up my heart to, as when I was a child."

Did Jesus come to visit you often?

"Every time he went to Jerusalem, he stopped by our house. It was my responsibility to prepare the meal and set the table. Mary sat at his feet listening to him. It was for this reason that one time I complained to Jesus that Mary wasn't helping me."

And Jesus reprimanded you instead of Mary. Doesn't that seem absurd to you?

"With the words, 'Mary has chosen the better part,' Jesus made me understand that the soul is more valuable than the body. Jesus was our friend, our great friend, and our home was his home. I wasn't offended, because I interpreted that observation as a polite hint not to overdo things, since we were among friends and I didn't have to worry so much. But I could never stay still. I've been like that since I was little."

What was the most common food in your country at that time?

"Fish. Small fish were either dried, salted and eaten with bread, or roasted on the fire and eaten fresh."

And what about fruit?

"There were grapes, figs and dates. There were also olives, pomegranates, almonds and pistachio nuts. There were always plenty of vegetables, including beans, lentils, peas, onions, cucumbers and melons. Butter wasn't used much, because it wasn't easy to preserve in that hot climate. But cheese and yogurt were popular. Fried eggs were the obligatory dish on the farms."

How did the women dress?

"They wore big tunics which they sometimes covered with a cloak and hood. Fabrics made of wool were used for winter, and linen fabrics were used for summer. Cotton and silk weren't used as often. Mixed fabrics of linen and wool were prohibited by law."

Were they colored fabrics?

"We women loved colors and

the dyers were kept very busy. There was a beautiful saffron yellow which was obtained from a springtime flower, the crocus; pink was made from the skin of the pomegranate; carmine was provided by an insect, a parasite of the oak tree; and purple came from a Mediterranean mollusk."

Did women use make-up and perfume?

"Jewish women were experts in the field of make-up for the face and eyes, and also nail polish. Perfume had a long history. One thousand years earlier, the camels of Sheba had brought great loads of it to Solomon. Judith put perfume

and make-up on before going to the Assyrian camp. Esther, too, put on perfume before going to see King Xerxes.... In Jerusalem, the women were authorized to spend one-tenth of their dowry on perfume."

Which perfumes were the most sought after?

"Jasmine and rose, the fresh cinnamon from the perfume of camphor and the very precious Indian lavender, for which there were substitutes and imitations."

Could you tell me about the episode when your brother died?

"On that occasion I saw Jesus cry. Lazarus had been dead for three days. He had been buried in a grave dug out of the hillside on the outskirts of Bethany. I begged Jesus to do something. I knew that nobody could bring people back to life, but I also knew that Jesus could do everything. And then the miracle happened."

Was Lazarus really dead?

"Do we really know what

death is? I'm a poor ignorant woman, but I've seen some people being born and I've seen some people die. Those who were born I saw and greeted, and those who died I never saw again. For me, this was life and death. Jesus turned this rule around. Lazarus had been dead for days, his body was already in an advanced state of decomposition . . . and yet I saw him walking around the house again. What is death?"

Is there an episode in the life of Jesus that especially impressed you?

"The one about the adulteress who was supposed to be stoned to death because our law decreed it. I've heard the story told so many times! And each time, I saw Jesus starting to scribble in the dust with his finger while those men continued to insist: should we stone her or not? Then he uttered the sentence, 'Let whoever is without sin among you be the first to throw a stone at her.'"

What happened to that woman?

"The men who were accusing her all went away in silence. Jesus and the woman were left in the middle of one of the temple courtyards. When he asked her, 'Has no one condemned you?' she replied, 'No one, Lord.' Jesus said, 'Neither do I condemn you. Go your way, and from now on sin no more.' I don't think that woman really knew who it was she was standing with, but she definitely had been saved by his forgiveness."

What did Jesus teach you?

"That there's a hierarchy of values. At the top, there's faith and spiritual concerns. Further down are the necessities of life and bodily concerns, including the need for food, clothing, a home and work."

You and Mary are revered as saints. Why is that?

"Mary, the contemplative one, had chosen the better part. Nevertheless, even though I worried about the less important part, I hadn't denied the best. Let's say that we were both 'promoted': Mary because of her interior life, and me because of my hard work, work that was motivated by the light of faith and the warmth of kindness."

Caiaphas, a Persecutor of Jesus

"So the cohort and their tribune and the attendants of the Jews seized Jesus and bound him and led him first to Annas—he was the father-in-law of Caiaphas, who was high priest that year— for it was Caiaphas who had advised the Jews that it was better for one man to die for the people."
(John 18:12-14)

Who are you?
"My name is Joseph, more commonly known as Caiaphas, the high priest."

What did it mean to be a high priest in Jerusalem?
"I was the leader of all the Hebrews, not only in matters of religion but also in civil matters. The high priest was chosen from among the members of the priestly families who were particularly influential."

Were you elected by the Sanhedrin, the highest Hebrew court?
"I was named by the Roman procurator Valerian Gratus in the year 18 and then confirmed by Pontius Pilate."

Did you share your important duty with Annas?
"Annas was my father-in-law. I had married one of his daughters. Annas had been high priest before me, but he was deposed by the Romans. Then his son Eleazar took over most of the duties, but after two years he was deposed, too, and I arrived on the scene. But even

though both of them had been deposed, they kept the title 'high priest' and belonged to the Sanhedrin."

How was the Sanhedrin formed?

"It was made up of seventy-one persons. There weren't only priests. There were the elders, who belonged to the most important families in Jerusalem. There were also the Pharisees and scribes, experts in law and theology."

How did a trial take place at the Sanhedrin?

"First, the *Shemà*, the great Hebrew prayer, was recited; it immediately gave a special solemnity to the hearing. Then the facts were set forth, along with any circumstances that might increase or lessen the person's degree of guilt, and the witnesses were heard. If there was only one piece of evidence and it was favorable to the defendant, he was acquitted. To condemn him, instead, there had to be at least two pieces of evidence. In the less serious cases, the number of members who had to be present was quite small—only twenty-three."

Were there also defense attorneys?

"No. The defendant himself and the witnesses in his favor saw to the defense, after which the vote for the verdict took place. For the death sentence, an absolute majority of votes, plus two, was required. But the death sentence could not be carried out by the Sanhedrin. The last word was always up to the Roman procurator."

Could anyone be a witness in a trial?

"Not women, slaves, the insane or children. The blind, deaf-mutes and illiterate persons were excluded, as well as criminals and perjurers. And that's not all. The law didn't admit the testimony of people of questionable morality, people who were notoriously addicted to gambling and those who were known for lying. Also excluded were the parents and relatives of the defendant. The witnesses were very important and decisive in the trial. Even when the defendant pleaded guilty, the confirmation of two witnesses was necessary to condemn him. False testimony was severely punished, with the same penalty that was to be set for the accused."

What were the penalties that the Sanhedrin inflicted?

"The most serious crime in the eyes of the law—punishable by death—was a crime against religion. For other crimes (property damage, thefts, acts of violence toward one's family or immoral acts), various penalties were given, including prison, beating and expulsion from the religious community. Another example: killing a thief who had entered one's house at night was not considered homicide. It was, though, if the thief was killed during the day, because in that case an arrest would have been possible."

Tell me about those tragic days.

"In Jerusalem they were preparing for the feast of Passover. The Roman procurator, Pontius Pilate, had arrived from Caesarea. He had brought with him reinforcements that were ready to intervene whenever necessary. The city had filled up with pilgrims who had come from every part of the world to celebrate the most important feast of the Hebrews. Herod Antipas, the governor of Galilee, had also arrived in Jerusalem with his retinue."

Why did you resort to deceit in order to capture Jesus?

"The Nazarene was always surrounded by people. Everywhere he went, he was pro-

tected by a crowd. There was danger of creating disorder, of causing a revolt. It was necessary to catch him by surprise, away from the people, possibly on the outskirts of town at night."

And was it at this point that Judas entered on the scene?
"Judas knew Jesus' moves perfectly. He offered to deliver him to us without too much commotion, in exchange for a little money. Precise agreements were made with him about the place, the time and the signal, and the arrest took place with maximum speed and efficiency."

Why did you propose the death penalty for Jesus?
"After his capture, the Nazarene had been brought to my house. As head of the Sanhedrin, I did nothing else but listen to the witnesses. The evidence didn't coincide, so I commanded Jesus to say whether he really was the Messiah and the Son of God. He answered yes, he was."

So then what did you do?
"It was blasphemy. I yelled, 'Why do we still need witnesses?!' That man had offended God, and according to our law he had to be sentenced to death."

Without the clear testimony of witnesses? And then you handed Jesus over to Pontius Pilate. Was it out of fear or to gain favor with Rome, or did you think you would become stronger in the Sanhedrin?
"As I said before, the death penalty had to be confirmed and carried out by the Romans. There was no doubt as to Jesus' guilt. He claimed to be the Son of God. He was dangerous and blasphemous."

Why dangerous?
"The crowd followed him and many people said that he performed miracles. He also spoke about a new law of love, and he claimed that all people, even pagans, are children of God. There was the risk that

the law of Moses and civil order would be disturbed. And there's another detail that's not always taken into account. It took very little to disrupt the order that reigned in Judea. Along with disorder there was the danger of heavier intervention on the part of Rome. In fact, later events proved me right. About forty years later, when the people rebelled, it was the ruin of Jerusalem and of all the Hebrews."

Why did you also persecute the apostles and the disciples of Jesus?
"They were dangerous people. Their preaching clashed with our law."

The little information we have

THE SANHEDRIN AND THE HIGH PRIESTS

The Sanhedrin decided on Jesus' arrest and was the first authority to sentence him to death. But what exactly was the Sanhedrin?

It was the Jewish council that exercised religious power. It also exercised some civil power in Judea.

Instituted probably in the second century B.C., the Sanhedrin acquired importance especially during foreign rule. It also had the function of a Hebrew court, but without the power to impose the death penalty. The sentence given to Jesus was therefore worthless and could not be carried out. Only the Roman procurator could have someone put to death.

There were seventy-one members of the Sanhedrin and they were grouped into three classes: the chief priests, the elders and the scribes, the latter being the scholars, the law experts. The elders were the members who were seen most often in society; they were wealthy lay persons. The chief priests included the current high priest (who presided over the Sanhedrin), former high priests, and members of influential priestly families. From these was chosen the person destined to have the highest religious authority in Israel.

The first high priest was Aaron, whose successor was Eleazar. At that time, and for many centuries afterward, the appointment was for life. Things changed under the rule of the Syrian king Antiochus IV Epiphanes (175-164 B.C.). He began to discharge the high priests, replacing them with people of his own liking. Again in Roman times, the top figure of the religious hierarchy of Israel was appointed by the civil power. Caiaphas, for example, was designated high priest by the Roman procurator Valerian Gratus in A.D. 18. He remained in office for eighteen years until A.D. 36, an exceptionally long leadership for that era. This can only be explained by Caiaphas' cooperative attitude toward the Romans.

from Flavius Josephus and the evangelists depicts you as a weak man with no feelings for religion or justice. In short, a servant to the Romans....

"I behaved the way all the other high priests did. I only had the misfortune of occupying that post during the life of Jesus."

You stayed in office for eighteen years. That was unusual, don't you think?

"It was because I was a faithful servant of the law."

Wasn't it because of your thirst for power?

"I acted for the religious interests of my people."

With the other priests, you persuaded the crowd to prefer Barabbas, you sneered at Jesus on the cross, you requested Pilate to put the guard at the grave and you paid the soldiers so they would keep quiet about the resurrection and wouldn't spread the news about the disappearance of the body. Why all this?

"I already told you, that man was dangerous. In Jerusalem at that time, things weren't bad. It's true that there was Roman rule, but the power was in our hands. The Romans worried about maintaining order and collecting taxes, but we had the administration of justice and public matters. We were really the ones in command."

A group of Jewish scholars in the twentieth century did a "rerun" of Jesus' trial. Every single one voted for his acquittal. What do you say?

"After 2,000 years, things are seen in a different light. It's not easy to understand what was happening to us at that time."

Pontius Pilate, the One Who Condemned Jesus

"Now when Pilate saw that he was doing no good, but instead a riot was beginning, he took water and washed his hands in full view of the crowd and said, 'I'm innocent of this man's blood! See to it yourselves!' And in answer the whole people said, 'His blood be upon us, and upon our children!' Then he released Barabbas to them, but he had Jesus scourged and handed him over to be crucified."

(Matthew 27:24-26)

What were the duties of a Roman procurator?

"The procurator was the official with full power who governed the subject nation in the name of the emperor. He saw to the interests of Rome and sent the taxes to the emperor. Because of this, he was very powerful and was the head of the occupying army. In addition, he had to be an able politician to maintain a good relationship with the local authorities."

When were you made governor of Judea?

"Not only of Judea, but also of Samaria. It was the year 779 since the founding of Rome. According to your calculations, it was A.D. 26. I didn't go there of my own will, because it was a second-class Roman position."

Was life easy in Judea?

"It was anything but easy. There were many small armed revolts against Rome that had to be put down continually. And I've never understood that religion of theirs, with only one God, just as I didn't understand why images of our emperor were strictly prohibited. In addition, I didn't do well politically, because I despised the great priests, who were nevertheless cordial toward me. I commanded the respect of the army, however."

Did you have many soldiers under you?

"Very few, and they were almost all auxiliary recruits in Samaria and Syria. But to make up for it, they were well-armed. If riots broke out, the legions that were stationed in Syria intervened to restore order."

What was the Roman Empire like at that time?

"The authority of Rome extended from Scotland to the borders of Persia, from the Atlantic Ocean to the Black Sea. It included within its boundaries tens if not hundreds of different peoples, each with their own culture, their own language and their own religious and legal customs."

Jesus wasn't a violent man. Why did you sentence him to death?

"Because a wild crowd asked me to. I had no choice. Either I ordered my soldiers to go ahead with a massacre or I sacrificed him. In reality, Jesus was sentenced to death by the Sanhedrin, the great council that administered power over the people. At that time the high priest was Caiaphas, a despicable character."

In history, the responsibility is yours, isn't it?

"Yes, I know. That Jesus ruined my life. My political career was practically finished that day. I never slept a night in peace again. In my sleep, I saw his eyes again and heard his voice saying, 'My kingdom is not of this world....'"

Did you try to save him?

"Yes, in every way possible, because he was innocent. At first, I sent him to Herod Antipas, who in those days was in Jerusalem. Antipas, the son of Herod the Great, was the governor of Galilee, Jesus' homeland. He was therefore competent to judge him. But Herod was too shrewd to compromise himself on that matter. He already had that preacher named John the Baptist on his conscience. After laughing at Jesus, he sent him back to me."

You declared him innocent and then you had him whipped. What kind of justice did you practice?

"Listen, I would have set Jesus free just to spite the priests. But there was a serious problem of public order to be resolved. The city had been stirred up and was in turmoil. There was the risk of disorder and riots. Then I tried my luck with the whipping...."

What do you mean?

"The sight of that punishment might have calmed the crowd. In fact, after the beating, I showed them Jesus, bleeding and full of wounds. But instead of calming down, the crowd became more excited than ever. They cried aloud for Jesus' crucifixion."

Was it at this point that you resorted to Barabbas?

"Yes. There was the custom of

releasing a condemned man at Passover. I offered the crowd a choice between the revolutionary Barabbas and Jesus. It didn't work; and yet Barabbas was an enemy of Rome and deserved the cross."

Was the death sentence legitimate according to Roman law?

"I really don't think so. And from what I learned later, Jesus should have been acquitted even on the basis of Hebrew law. It was a major error. And at the bottom of everything there was a religious tiff among the Jewish leaders."

Don't you think it was against Rome's interests to let these people trample on Roman law and authority?

"No, the imperial politics of Rome were clear. In the occupied territories, local customs, traditions and beliefs could never be touched as long as they didn't injure the empire."

What was the meaning of that basin of water that you had brought to you before you ordered Jesus' death?

"I used it to wash my hands and thereby to ease my conscience, but above all to let Rome know about my correct behavior. I washed my hands so the blame would be put on the Judeans, and I wanted Rome to know it. The emperor had so many spies in Judea."

You have nothing else to say to justify yourself?

"What good would it do? I can be proud of one thing, though. I broke an enforced custom and had Jesus' body given over to a certain Joseph of Arimathea instead of letting it be thrown into the common ditch for the condemned. Then, strangely, they told me that Jesus had risen. Nonsense! My wife always repeated it to me, though—maybe to make my nightmares go away. I was sure that the sentence had been thoroughly carried out."

Were you there at the cross?

"It wasn't a spectacle that interested me. But I received a detailed report. At nine o'clock in the morning Jesus was nailed to the cross between two thieves. In the afternoon he weakened for a moment under the torture, and murmured, 'My God, why have you forsaken me?' At three o'clock he breathed his last."

Why have Roman historians ignored the figure of Jesus?

"For them, he was a traveling preacher confined to an obscure corner of the Roman Empire. Tacitus mentions Jesus, but only to explain the origin of the Christians who were put to death by Nero."

How do you judge yourself?

"Definitely guilty, because I humiliated and betrayed the justice of Rome and I threw mud on the noble figure of the Roman official. But I have many excuses. So many legends, all positive, have been created about me, which show that people, even Christians, haven't considered me in a completely negative way. One of these legends says that the risen Jesus appeared to me, telling me to not torment myself anymore for the sentence that I was forced to inflict upon him. Another legend claimed that I converted and became a valuable witness of Jesus' innocence and defended his resurrection. In the Coptic Church, I'm venerated as a saint."

Eusebius says that you committed suicide; others say that you were beheaded under Nero; and still others say that you died a good Christian. What do you say?
"I died in secret, trying to have others forget me. After ten years of living in Judea, I had been relieved of my duties. It was after the incident on Mt. Gerizim."

What happened on Mt. Gerizim?
"A rumor had spread in Samaria that there was a treasure hidden on the mountain, a treasure of great religious importance, none other than the sacred vessels of Moses. This rumor made many people run to the area. Fearing disorder, I

THE ROMAN EMPIRE AT THE TIME OF JESUS

At the time of Jesus, the Roman Empire had not yet reached its maximum expansion (which would happen in the following century under Trajan). Nevertheless, it controlled the entire Mediterranean basin. Augustus put an end to wars of conquest and dedicated himself to the reorganization of political structures. The subject territories outside of the Italian peninsula were divided into provinces. Gaul had four of them (Aquitania, Lugdunum, Narbo and Belgica), the Iberian peninsula had three (Lusitania, Tarraconensis and Baetica). Then there were Sicily, Sardinia, Raetia, Noricum, Achaea, Macedonia, Cyprus, Cyrene, Pannonia, Dalmatia, Mesia, Asia, Bithynia, Galatia, Pamphylia, Syria, Africa and Numidia.

There were also many territories which depended on Rome, but kept a certain autonomy. Their rulers, however, had to report to the emperor. That was the case with Thrace, Cappadocia, Lycia, Pontus, Mauritania and some other Asiatic and African regions. Egypt, on the other hand, was a kind of personal property of the emperor.

The holy land also represented a special situation. Subjected by Pompey in 63 B.C., it retained a certain autonomy. In 37 B.C., it was entrusted to King Herod the Great, and after his death it was divided among three of his sons. However, after A.D. 6, it was directly ruled by a Roman procurator, dependent perhaps on the imperial ambassador to Syria.

There were in fact two types of provinces in the Roman Empire: those that were managed by the Roman senate through officials, and those that were managed by the emperor through ambassadors. The frontier provinces in particular, were "imperial." For reasons of safety the constant presence of the army was required. Syria and the holy land occupied a very important geographical position. They were inhabited by restless populations that had to be constantly kept under observation by the emperor through his trusted men.

---

sent some troops to the top of the mountain. Even though it was forbidden, the crowd began to climb the mountain slopes. Then the soldiers took up their weapons and there was a massacre. The Samaritans, who were highly visible in Rome, made me pay for it. I left Judea and got out of political life."

Do you have any regrets?
"Yes, I regret having become a symbol of meanness, when I'm really history's most illustrious victim of politics."

Barabbas, the Robber "Saved" by Jesus

"Now at the festival it was the governor's custom to release to the crowd any one prisoner they wanted. At that time they had a notorious prisoner named Barabbas.... Now the chief priests and elders persuaded the crowd to ask for Barabbas [but] to have Jesus killed."
(Matthew 27:15-16, 20)

What does your name mean?
"In Aramaic it means 'son of the father.'"

Who are you?
"I know I'm not liked, but I'm innocent. I had nothing to do with that production orchestrated by Pontius Pilate."

But Jesus was the one who ended up in your place on the cross.

"Yes, that cross was definitely mine. I had already been condemned to death."

What did you do?
"Revolts were common in Jerusalem, and riots and disorder were everyday events. A person was killed during a brawl, and they said that I was the one who did it."

Were you a violent man?
"I was a man of my time."

Did you have a regular trial?
"I'm not an expert on procedures and laws."

Who sentenced you?
"The Romans did, with a very quick trial that I don't remember many details about. I'm convinced that the death sentence had been decided from the moment the Roman soldiers captured me."

How was the death penalty to be carried out?
"According to Hebrew law, I would have been faced with stoning, fire or beheading. A fourth possibility was strangulation. But the Judeans, who were a subject people oppressed by the Romans, could not carry out capital punishment. So the Romans decided that I would end up on a cross. In a stinking prison, I waited to

PRISONS AND SLAVERY

When Jesus was tried and convicted, Barabbas was already in prison waiting to be executed as a robber, murderer and revolutionary.

At that time, prisons weren't the places of detention and isolation that they are today, where convicted persons serve out their sentences. They were simply places of custody for persons who were to be tried or executed. They were crowded gloomy dungeons where the accused and condemned were closed up with no regard for their health or human dignity.

It was, moreover, an era when human beings suffered many other atrocities. For example, slavery was practiced in all ancient civilizations, and great philosophers and thinkers even justified it. Slavery was maintained especially by wars. Prisoners of war became the "property" of whoever captured them.

It has been calculated that in Athens, at the height of its splendor (fifth century B.C.), there were more than 100,000 slaves. There were also many slaves in the Roman Empire, although the emperor Augustus ordered that families living in the city couldn't have more than twenty each.

Like everyone else, the Hebrews had practiced slavery from ancient times. Prisoners of war became slaves. Israelites would even become slaves to one another if they couldn't pay their debts or if, after robbing someone, they weren't able to return the stolen property. Hebrew law, however, greatly limited the rights of the owner. An Israelite slave couldn't be sold to foreigners. Every seventh year ("sabbatical year") the Israelite slaves had to be freed and their debts had to be canceled.

be beaten and roped or nailed to a cross. There was no hope for me."

Did you belong to the group of Zealots that fought to free your country from Roman occupation?
"The Zealots were patriots, good people. They were tired of those Romans, who didn't understand one word of our language."

How did the Romans behave?
"Like all the occupying troops, with arrogance and impudence. So many of my companions and friends had been reduced to slavery and ended up working in some other part of the huge Roman Empire. Whenever something happened, even just a slight protest against injustices, the soldiers arrived and they didn't make distinctions. They would take a group of Hebrews and load them on a ship. It didn't matter whether they were guilty or innocent."

What was Jerusalem like in your time?
"There was great confusion. The narrow streets were clogged with people, the air we breathed was what you would call polluted, the stink of the tanneries mixed with the aromas of incense and spices and

108

the foul odors from outdoor kitchens. The sounds included the calls of the water vendors and the bleating of the herds that were heading toward the temple. Every so often the uproar of the bazaar was broken by trumpet blasts that invited everyone to stop all their work for the ritual prayer pauses of the day."

Did you go to the temple sometimes?
"It wasn't a place that I liked to go to."

Why did the crowd prefer you, a murderer and a robber, to Jesus, who hadn't done anything bad?
"It was a surprise. When I was brought in front of the crowd, I saw that there was another man between the guards. His face was stained with blood but serene. I knew who he was; I had seen him once before. They spoke about him a lot in Judea, and I didn't understand why he had to be condemned. When the crowd shouted out my name, he didn't bat an eyelash. I jumped for joy and didn't even wonder whether Jesus was guilty or innocent. I only knew that a nightmare had ended for me."

Today, Barabbas is synonymous with wickedness.

"I was no saint. But I'll tell you again that if Jesus ended up on the cross, it wasn't my fault. In fact, I was the first man whom Jesus saved with his death."

Did you know what Jesus preached?
"Of course. Everyone knew a few phrases of his. They were things that I didn't understand. They seemed outside of reality. I was a man of action. I reacted to violence with vio-

lence, I faced arrogance with arrogance."

Did you know who the apostles were?
"Don't ask me difficult questions, please."

What do you think of Pontius Pilate?
"Strange guy! In Jerusalem there was the custom of releasing a man condemned to death at Passover. The Roman governor was definitely on Jesus' side, not mine. He tried playing the Barabbas card and it didn't work. He doesn't have a good name in history, either."

Two thieves also ended up on the cross beside Jesus. Were they your friends?
"I knew them."

Some writers, including the Swede Pär Lagervist (a Nobel Prize winner), have imagined that after Jesus' death you became a Christian and died a martyr. However, according to them, you never understood Jesus' message of love and you would even have killed others in order to defend Jesus' doctrine and his followers.
"Those are legends. Some people have even claimed that I had the ferocity and the innocence of an animal."

Nicodemus, a Pharisee Friend of Jesus

"Now there was a man of the Pharisees named Nicodemus, a ruler of the Jews. He came to Jesus at night and said to him, 'Rabbi, we know that you're a teacher come from God, because no one can do the signs you're doing unless God is with him.'"
(John 3:1-2)

Why did you run to Calvary?
"There was a friend of mine there, an innocent man who had been executed by the Romans. He needed burial. I had brought more than one hundred pounds of myrrh and aloes to spread on Jesus' body, according to the custom."

And you managed to carry it?
"My servants took care of that."

When did you see Jesus for the first time?
"I saw him at the temple when he caused that great scandal."

What scandal?
"When he whipped the merchants who were carrying on their business in the 'court of the Gentiles.' It was a spacious

hall in the temple that anyone could have access to, even non-believers and pagans. That area had become a huge market. There were all kinds of vendors, moneychangers, animals for sacrifice.... In the middle of all that uproar, Jesus appeared, carrying a whip made out of rope. He started to hit the merchants' tables and overturn the animal cages. He was yelling, 'Get out of here! Take this stuff away and don't make my Father's house a marketplace!' It was an extraordinary spectacle."

When did you see Jesus again?
"I went to visit him at night to talk with him. I was very religious and continuously tormented by the desire for truth. I wanted to bring my people back to the purity and greatness of the past. I was anxious to catch even the most subtle indications and clues. Had the Messiah finally arrived? I had to check whether or not Jesus was part of the divine plan."

Why did you go to visit him at night?
"Because of caution, not fear. My family was one of the richest in Jerusalem. I was part of the Sanhedrin and belonged to the group of the Pharisees. I was a great leader of the Judeans. Jesus was not appreciated much by people in power. They considered him a dangerous and fanatic agitator who could compromise the unstable political situation of Judea."

And what was your impression of Jesus?
"A great friendship was immediately established between us. After hearing his first words, I had no more doubts that he was a teacher who came from God. He was almost certainly the Messiah who had been announced in the Sacred Scriptures by the prophets. I wanted to know from him if it was enough to be an Israelite in order to participate in the good things that the Messiah would bring."

What did Jesus say to you?
"He explained some interesting things of extraordinary theological richness. Then he said, 'You're a teacher in Israel and you don't know these things?'"

Was Jesus' trial a regular one?
"The most elementary procedural rules were discarded. That wicked man Caiaphas, who was stirred up by his father-in-law Annas, had already decided to rid himself of the Nazarene. He was just looking for a pretext to do it. It was a farce. I was strongly opposed to the sentence. My word usually had weight, but on that occasion it fell on deaf ears. Everyone was excited and in a hurry to conclude the 'Jesus case.' And that's how that disgraceful torture started. Jesus was led to Calvary like a defenseless sheep to slaughter."

When you went to Calvary, who was near the cross?
"There were the soldiers who had cast dice for Jesus' cloak. Joseph of Arimathea's servants were taking the body down from the cross. There were also some women who were crying. Among them there was certainly Mary, Jesus' mother. I think I caught a glimpse of John, one of the apostles whom I knew quite well."

How did funerals take place in Israel?
"The law established that no body should be left without a burial, not even the body of the worst enemy or the body of a man sentenced to death. There was a very strict ceremony. When a person died, the body was washed and anointed with aromatic herbs and perfumes. It wasn't a real embalming, but

rather a kind of homage to the deceased."

What was the perfume that was used the most?

"Lavender with myrrh and aloes. Some of the aromatic herbs were poured on the body and the rest was poured on the inside of the grave. After being washed and perfumed, the body was then wrapped in a sheet. A shroud covered the face, and the hands and feet were tied with strips of linen. The body was then brought to the last resting place by relatives and friends, who wept aloud in sorrow. Even the poorest man, if his wife died, had to call to the funeral at least two flute players and at least one 'wailing' woman who united her cries with those of the relatives. There was even the ritual of the tearing of the clothes."

And what happened after the funeral?

"The body of the deceased was no longer an object of particular attention. In fact, in order to create more space, after some time the remains were taken from the tomb (something that happens even in your time) and placed in a charnel house."

Tell me about Jesus' funeral.

"For Jesus we had to move

quickly. The spies of the priests of the Sanhedrin were making sure that everything proceeded according to Hebrew law. But, above all, they wanted the ceremony to end before sundown."

What was the meaning of that inscription on the cross above Jesus' head? Was it another form of mockery?

"It was the reason for the condemnation. It was written on a small board covered with

white paint, to bring out the letters. Jesus had been condemned because he had proclaimed himself king of the Jews. The inscription on the cross read, 'Jesus the Nazarene, King of the Jews,' abbreviated in Latin as I.N.R.I., that is, *Iesus Nazarenus Rex Iudaeorum.* The inscription was in three languages including Aramaic, the language spoken in my country; Greek, a

112

very widespread language in the East; and Latin, the official language of the Roman Empire. In Aramaic the inscription read *Jeshua Nazoraja Malka Dejehudaje*. This writing caused a small incident between Pontius Pilate and the priests of the Sanhedrin."

What incident was that?
"The priests were annoyed and wanted to modify the inscription to read: 'The one who called himself King of the Jews.' The Roman governor brusquely sent them away. That inscription was a Roman juridical document to be recorded in the archives. Therefore it was impossible to change even one letter."

Could you tell me about your family?
"They died in the course of the desperate Jewish revolt against the Romans, which led to the total destruction of Jerusalem."

Did you write a Gospel?
"They attributed one to me, the one that bears my name. But it's a false Gospel; it was only written to make Pontius Pilate seem innocent."

According to you, was Pontius Pilate guilty?
"I would acquit him because of

SCHOOL IN THE HOLY LAND

In Old Testament times the Hebrews didn't really have schools. Children were taught in the family, especially about religion and the history and traditions of Israel. Boys also had to learn a trade from their fathers, while girls learned domestic chores from their mothers, such as baking bread, spinning and weaving.

After the Babylonian exile, synagogues sprang up. They were places where the Hebrews who lived far from Jerusalem gathered on the Sabbath to listen to biblical readings and to pray. Then schools were started in the synagogues where boys were educated, starting at the age of six. The example also came from other ancient peoples like the Egyptians. They had schools—which were almost always connected to the temples—where youths studied grammar and literature, natural sciences, mathematics, geography and astronomy.

In the synagogue schools the main subject was the Mosaic law, but other topics were not neglected.

The teachers were scribes, also called "doctors of the law" or "rabbis." At the time of Jesus, the Greek scholastic system had become famous and had been adopted throughout the Roman Empire. It also made its influence felt in the holy land and even more in Hebrew communities spread throughout the world.

According to this system, it was felt necessary to educate a boy's body as well as his mind. Therefore, along with grammar, rhetoric, poetry, dramatic art, music and philosophy, physical education was taught as well.

---

insufficient proof."

Would you do anything differently?

"I recognized the Messiah before anyone else did. What more could I have asked for?"

Joseph of Arimathea, A Secret Disciple

"Now after these things Joseph of Arimathea asked Pilate—since he was a disciple of Jesus, but a secret one for fear of the Jews—to let him take Jesus' body, and Pilate let him. So he came and took his body."
(John 19:38)

In a modern encyclopedia, under your name we read, "Secret disciple of Jesus, to whom he gave burial." Who are you?

"A rich landowner, originally from Arimathea, a village about eighteen and a half miles from Jerusalem. I was a member of the Sanhedrin, the highest religious and civil assembly of the Hebrew people."

Was it the head of the Sanhedrin who ordered Jesus' arrest?

"Jesus' arrest was ordered by Annas, not by the high priest Caiaphas. In fact, Annas was the real head of the Sanhedrin, the real Jewish leader of Jerusalem and Judea. Formerly a high priest, he had been deposed by the Romans. In an-

cient times, the appointment of the high priest was for life, but when the Romans arrived in my country, they started to appoint the head of the Sanhedrin. Whoever paid the most got the job. It was the relatives of Annas who built up the position. And do you know who Caiaphas was? He was the son-in-law of Annas, whose daughter he had married."

"Secret disciple." What does that mean? That you were afraid...?
"I wasn't afraid and I proved that immediately after Jesus' death when I hurried to the Roman governor to ask to have Jesus' body delivered to me. I didn't see any close friends of Jesus on that occasion. I was a secret sympathizer of the Messiah, and I'll explain to you why. If anyone had found out about it, I would surely have been excluded from the Sanhedrin. That group was formed mostly by Hebrews who were Roman sympathizers and benefited from their political power. Caiaphas, Annas and the other priests wanted things in Judea to remain as they were. Jesus spoke about a new kingdom, and so he automatically became 'dangerous.' He excited the crowd and could start hotbeds of revolt with the consequence of

heavier interventions on the part of the occupying troops."

So the Zealots, who wanted the liberty of your country, weren't favored by Jerusalem's wealthy class, either?
"They were considered extremely dangerous revolutionaries. Everyone wanted the liberation of Judea, but there were two sides, that of the Zealots, which was supported by humble people and which advocated armed combat, and that of the upper classes (priests, wealthy landowners, merchants and doctors of the law), who feared that a rebellion would bring about the destruction of Jerusalem by the Roman legions. This actually happened later on."

Could you tell me about Jesus' trial?
"What can I tell you? It was a farce because the death sentence had already been ordained by Annas and Caiaphas. When Jesus said he was the Son of God, Caiaphas tore his clothes, shouting that Jesus was a blasphemer and deserved death."

Were all the members of the Sanhedrin against Jesus?
"Nicodemus and I were energetically opposed to the injus-

tice of the trial. When Caiaphas decided on Jesus' death, not all of the seventy-one members of the Sanhedrin were present. How could anyone know whether those who were absent would have been favorable to the sentence or to Jesus' acquittal? I can say that Gamaliel, a wise and educated person, was not present at the trial. Afterward, Gamaliel advised his colleagues not to persecute those who were announcing that Jesus was Christ, that is, the Messiah."

Why had the Sanhedrin also sentenced two thieves, who were crucified beside Jesus?
"It was the Romans, not the Hebrew court, who condemned those men. They were revolutionaries who were judged and condemned after Jesus, on the same morning. For the Romans, the death sentence was carried out without delay on the same day it was issued."

When you went to the governor's palace to get Jesus' body, what did Pontius Pilate say to you?
"He was amazed that Jesus was already dead. It was three o'clock in the afternoon. Usually, the torture on the cross lasted longer. The two thieves died later. To speed up their

death, the soldiers broke their legs."

Pontius Pilate didn't have any objections?
"After being informed by the head of the guards that Jesus was really dead, he told me that I could take his body down from the cross."

What kind of impression did Pontius Pilate make on you?
"I had the impression that he didn't consider Jesus a real political enemy and that he had pronounced the sentence reluctantly."

Why did you want to bury Jesus?
"To prevent him from ending up in the common grave, the one for executed people. Roman law didn't forbid relatives and friends from giving a normal burial to those who were executed. Nor did Jewish law forbid it. In fact, in my time, acts of kindness were part of the duties of honor of the Sanhedrin's members. Emergency burials was also part of this. Actually the Scriptures urged people to bury those who were executed. I'll read you the piece: 'If a man commits a crime worthy of death and you put him to death and hang him on a tree, his body must not remain hung on the

tree the whole night, but you will bury him the same day because he is a curse of God and you will not contaminate the country which your Lord gives you as a heritage.' Therefore, nobody could criticize me for this proper and obligatory action."

Who went to Calvary with you?
"My servants. Then Nicodemus also arrived with his servants. He brought a mixture of myrrh and aloes to wash and anoint the body of Jesus. We had to hurry. After we had taken the body down from the cross, we wrapped it in a sheet...."

Why did you have to hurry?
"Sunset was coming and after that nobody could do anything. It was Friday, the eve of Passover. At sunset all work had to be interrupted. So we hurried toward my private tomb, which I had dug in the rock in the garden near Calvary. After we carefully set the body down on the tomb's slab of rock, we spread aromatic herbs around. Finally the huge rock was rolled in front of the entrance. Just at that moment the sun disappeared over the horizon. The Sabbath rest had begun."

Wasn't there any funeral procession?
"There was no procession. The apostles were worried about ending up on crosses themselves and had hidden. Some

women had followed us, but they didn't come near the tomb."

Is it true that Judas Iscariot gave back the money, the price of the betrayal?
"Judas showed up at the temple and threw the thirty silver shekels on the floor, shouting that Jesus was innocent. Then he ran away. Desperation was on his face. That money had become contaminated in the hands of a traitor and it couldn't be returned to the temple treasury. Therefore it was given to a potter in exchange for a piece of land to be used for the burial of foreigners. That field was called 'Field of Blood.'"

Legends have sprung up about you....
"Yes. According to tradition, at the time of Charlemagne my remains were transported from Jerusalem to Moyenmoustier in France and were then taken away by monks."

Don't you also appear in the legend of the Knights of the Round Table?
"That's the 'search for the Holy Grail,' which was started in medieval times and has fascinated generations. Even today there are still some people who continue to search for the

FUNERAL CUSTOMS

The Hebrews had always had great respect for the dead, even though they hadn't always believed in the afterlife. In general, the early Israelites believed that the deceased went down to *Sheòl*, an underground place of rest which was dark and lifeless. Only gradually did the idea develop that God wouldn't abandon his children to such a sad destiny and that he would lead them to a new life of peace and joy. At the time of Jesus, nearly all the Jewish people, with the exception of the Sadducees, believed that their deceased would be raised up and that righteous people would have a blessed life "in Abraham's bosom." Wicked people instead, would be thrown "into the fire of Gehenna (hell)." Whether or not they believed in the resurrection, however, the Hebrews of Jesus' time carried out precise obligations in regard to the deceased. They closed the eyes, washed the body, wrapped it in strips of cloth and brought it to the place of burial. Mourning normally lasted seven days. During that time the people cried and made a conspicuous show of their sorrow. They fasted, tore their clothes, sprinkled ashes on their heads, walked barefoot....

The poor were buried in ditches dug in the open countryside and covered with stone slabs. The wealthy, on the other hand, had large family tombs with ample funeral chambers in which various burial niches were carved into the walls. The entrance to such a tomb was always quite low, so low, in fact, that one had to enter on all fours. It was sealed off by a boulder or a slab of rock made to roll or slide along a special groove.

In Jerusalem, these family tombs were outside the walls of the city. This was also true of the one where Jesus was buried. All the tombs were painted white so people would notice them and not touch them. Any contact with the dead made them "impure," that is, unable to participate in acts of worship.

Holy Grail. The word 'grail' means cup. Some say that I collected the last drops of Christ's blood in a cup and then brought the sacred chalice with me to Britain and to Provence, where I preached the Gospel. But that's all a legend."

Would you like to say anything else?
"I was a secret disciple, but not a secret one forever. I'm glad I could be close to Jesus in his last hours."

Stephen, the First Christian Martyr

"Stephen, a man richly blessed by God and full of power, performed great miracles and wonders among the people.... Stephen, full of the Holy Spirit, looked up to heaven and saw God's glory and Jesus standing at the right side of God. 'Look!' he said. 'I see heaven opened and the Son of Man standing at the right side of God!' With a loud cry the Council members covered their ears with their hands. Then they all rushed at him at once, threw him out of the city, and stoned him."

(Acts 6:8; 7:55-57)

Why do they call you the first martyr?

"They consider me the first martyr of the Christian faith, the first man who was killed for Christ. I belonged to the group of deacons. We had the responsibility of helping the apostles by assisting the most needy people of the community."

The famous "seven helpers?"

"Exactly. My deacon companions were Philip, Prochorus, Nicanor, Timon, Parmenas, and Nicolaus of Antioch. The Christian community of Jerusalem had grown notably. Disagreements and tension arose because some of the Greek-speaking widows were neglected in the daily distribution of food. The apostles had suggested that the community name seven helpers with the task of organizing meals."

Was that your job?

"Not only that. We deacons also took care of administrative matters and helped the apostles with missionary work, with preaching."

You mentioned the "Greek-speaking widows." Was Greek your first language?

"Yes. I was a Hellenist."

What does that mean?

"The Hellenists were Hebrews who had grown up in Greek-speaking regions—that is, in pagan regions. A sharp distinction was made between the Hellenists and the Hebrews who were natives of the holy land and spoke Aramaic."

What was the difference?

"There was little difference on the surface. The Hellenists read the Scriptures in Greek, and the Aramaic-speaking Hebrews read them in Hebrew. Deeper down.... Well, the temple and the law were less central for us."

Where did these Hellenists come from?

"From the time of the exile onward, a great many Hebrews had spread out to various parts of the world, moving into large centers of trade, and so forth. Being attached to their own religious identity, they had always maintained close contact with Jerusalem. They paid taxes in order to send funds to the temple. The Hebrews in Egypt, for example, no longer knew Hebrew; they spoke Greek. Many of these Hellenists later returned to the land of their ancestors. In Jerusalem, Hellenistic synagogues sprang up, where the liturgy and teaching were conducted in Greek. I was one of these

Hellenists. I preached the word of Jesus among my people. My name in Greek means 'crown.'"

Did you get along well with the apostles?

"I think so. But don't ask me who I liked the most. In my eyes they were all equal."

Why were you dragged before the Sanhedrin?

"I had been reported because of a speech I had given in the synagogue of the Freedmen, which was attended by Cyreneans, Alexandrians and natives of Cilicia and Asia. The Sanhedrin had me arrested and brought before them. False witnesses accused me of having spoken against the temple, the law of Moses and even God. I immediately understood the seriousness of situation. Those kinds of accusations required the death penalty."

How did you defend yourself?

"I spoke about the history of my Hebrew people, trying to show that the universal salvation brought by Jesus came from God. I didn't only try to defend myself. I also attacked, stating that the real guilty ones were my opponents. The temple was the most important thing for the Hebrew religion. But I reminded them that even before it existed, in the era of the patriarchs, true religion had been practiced. As far as the Law was concerned, I reminded them that the people of Israel themselves had opposed it at the time of Moses...."

You called those who were listening to you traitors and murderers....
"They were. They had persecuted the prophets, killed those who announced the coming of the Messiah and nailed Jesus to the cross."

Is it true that you had the temperament of John the Baptist?
"That seems like an exaggeration. It's true that I wasn't cautious or tactful. To use an expression of yours, 'I called a spade a spade.'"

Was it a regular trial?
"It was confusing and improper. While I was still speaking, they dragged me out of the building to a rocky area so as to carry out the death penalty."

But didn't the death sentence have to be confirmed by Roman authority?
"Of course, but that procedure wasn't always respected. A brief trial was simply followed by hanging or stoning."

What did stoning consist of?

"It was an ancient type of painful death. A person died under a hail of stones. Among the Hebrews, idolators, adulterers, blasphemers and violators of the Sabbath were condemned by the Mosaic law to stoning."

When the stones started to rain on you, what did you think?
"I knelt down and prayed to the Lord that he would receive my spirit. As the pain got worse, I cried out, 'Lord, don't hold this sin against them!'"

What year did you die?
"I don't know exactly by your reckoning. Jesus had been dead for a few years. It was probably the year 36."

Was Paul of Tarsus one of your executioners?
"That's what they say, but he didn't take part in the stoning. It seems he limited himself to looking after the cloaks of the others. Maybe he hadn't reached the legal age for throwing stones."

What twentieth-century person do you most admire?
"Father Maximilian Kolbe, the Polish priest who sacrificed his

life to save a man in a German concentration camp."

What were your best qualities?

"Tenacity and frankness."

Do you have any regrets?

"I don't remember complaining, even when the pain was excruciating."

Do you wish you had written a Gospel?

"Others did it very well, but I had a different mission."

Where are your remains buried?

"According to tradition, my relics were transported first to Constantinople and then, around 1100, to Venice, to the church of St. George the Elder."

You've inspired many painters. Which painting of your martyrdom do you like most?

"The fresco by Fra Angelico that is kept in the Vatican."

In the Divine Comedy, Dante presents you as a docile young man. Why is that?

"Maybe because of an historical error. I'm represented as a youth in Christian paintings, too."

MARTYRS AND "CONFESSORS"

Stephen is usually called "the first martyr" of Christianity. Later, James the Greater and almost all the other apostles suffered the same fate. The number of Jesus Christ's followers who were cruelly executed increased enormously during the persecutions that took place under various emperors, including Nero, Domitian, Trajan, Hadrian, Marcus Aurelius, Septimius Severus, Maximin, Decius, Valerian, Diocletian and Maximian.

What does "martyr" mean? The word is of Greek origin and literally means "witness." As such it was first used for the apostles, who were the direct witnesses of the life and teachings of Jesus.

Only later did people give the name "martyrs" to all who showed their unshakable faith by accepting unspeakable torture and death for the love of Jesus Christ.

Only those who were actually killed for their faith were martyrs. Instead, those who were persecuted and underwent great sufferings for the faith, without losing their lives, were called "confessors."

To be a martyr meant having the highest title of glory in the Church. The faithful immediately considered those who had shed their blood for Jesus to be powerful intercessors with God, since their souls had gone directly to heaven.

Martyrs' homes and tombs often became places of prayer and pilgrimage. The day of their martyrdom, called *dies natalis* (day of birth in heaven), was commemorated each year with great solemnity.

It's from the honor bestowed on the martyrs that the veneration of the saints had its beginning.

Is there a passage of the Gospel that especially fascinates you?
"The closing of the Gospel of Matthew, with the words of Jesus: 'I'll be with you all the days until the end of the age.'"

Simon the Magician, Peter's Rival

"A man named Simon lived there, who for some time had astounded the Samaritans with his magic. He claimed that he was someone great.... Simon saw that the Spirit had been given to the believers when the apostles placed their hands on them. So he offered money to Peter and John, and said, 'Give this power to me too, so that anyone I place my hands on will receive the Holy Spirit.' But Peter answered him, 'May you and your money go to hell, for thinking that you can buy God's gift with money!'"
(Acts 8:9, 18-20)

Where are you from?
"I'm from Samaria, like that good Samaritan who ran to help a Judean in trouble, even though he was an enemy."

Did you know Jesus?

"Not personally. I knew that he was a great man capable of incredible miracles. I should know what's great because I studied magic arts in Alexandria. That disciple of Jesus who was called Simon, like me, was also remarkable."

Are you talking about Peter?
"Yes. He was a magician, too, even though he met a terrible end under Nero. I should also say that, all things considered, his master, Jesus, disappointed me. As extraordinary as he was in performing miracles, I thought he would have released himself from the cross. Instead, he let himself be killed while calling out to his heavenly Father. Who knows which one of our gods he was referring to?"

Did you know Peter?
"Certainly. He was a fisherman by the name of Simon who called himself Peter. In fact, Jesus had given him that name: 'You are to be called Cephas, which means rock, and on this rock I will build my Church.' Another temple in this land of the Hebrews which already has temples, or in Rome where you can't even count them."

Jesus also said to Peter, "You will be a fisher of men...."

"And to win the faith of the people, he performed miracles, like John, another friend of his. They were called apostles and they performed wonders, even though their wonders weren't like those of Jesus. I really would have liked to do those. Jesus multiplied bread and fish, transformed water into wine and even raised the dead to life. Those were really miracles. I don't know who taught them to him. Not even my magic school in Alexandria could go that far. But these other two were good, too. By using their hands, Peter and John could cure the sick and do other things that I wasn't capable of."

So what happened?
"One day I went to them. I asked them, 'Why don't you sell your knowledge to me and teach me your magic arts?' They responded that their power came from God and could neither be sold nor taught. Faith was needed. Faith in God, in his son Jesus, in the Holy Spirit. I thought they wanted to raise the price. I wasn't able to convince them."

We call the act of making money on holy things "simony...."
"I really wanted to *give* money, not *take* it, even though it's true that I would have made more later."

If you didn't believe, why did you have yourself baptized?
"That happened before I knew Peter. A man named Philip had arrived in Samaria. He was a deacon, a kind of priest, I guess, and also a magician. He performed miracles and could heal the paralyzed and the crippled. He also spoke about a kingdom of God which wasn't well-defined. When he spoke, he fascinated people. In Samaria hundreds of people had themselves baptized by him. I was among them."

With the hope of snatching the secret of his miracles?
"Keep in mind that I could perform miracles, too. They called me 'the power of God.' And I also had followers, who even formed a sect called the Simonians."

And why did you escape from Samaria?
"I didn't escape. I liked to travel. After a long stay in Alexandria, in Egypt, where I taught magic arts, I settled in Rome. I became a popular and loved figure there, too. The Emperor Nero protected me and appreciated my art. I knew that Peter had also arrived in Rome after me. And another

competitor of mine was a certain Paul, who called himself Saul of Tarsus before converting to the Christian faith. Peter and Paul said that Jesus had risen. I didn't know whether to believe that or not. If he had succeeded, then he must have really been a great magician."

Were there many Christians in Rome?
"There were many Hebrews and quite a few Christians. Among them there was Peter, who acted as if he were the head of the Christians. I knew

that the Romans wanted to kill him. Nero had blamed the Christians for the terrible fire of Rome. I hoped they would catch him. He would be one less competitor."

Why were you so against Peter?
"The fact is that Peter gave me the greatest humiliation of my life."

What was that?
"Among my many arts, I also knew how to fly. Not like a bird, though. I didn't have

strong enough arms to move the flaps of my cloak as if they were wings. But I had studied birds in the sky and I had seen how they could slowly glide toward the ground. So I put on a huge cloak that was strong, yet light. I was light, too, tall and all bones, with long arms and legs. Inside the cloak I hid a device which kept my arms open and rigid when I spread them out wide."

And what does Peter have to do with that?

"One day I invited the Romans to the amphitheater so they could see me fly. Keep in mind that I had convinced many Christians that their faith wasn't worth anything. After my triumph, Peter would really find himself alone. I went up to the highest part of the arena and threw myself into the emptiness. I opened the cloak, the wind supported me and I began to descend slowly, giving the impression of flying. Suddenly, something happened. My cloak shook and then it became twisted. I fell suddenly, breaking a leg and my toes. The people went away laughing and the Christians who had been on my side went back to Peter. Then they told me that Peter had prayed hard to his God to make me fall. He won."

All these things that you've told me—are they really true?

"It's possible to read them in certain documents, which the Christians consider apocryphal, that is, not inspired by God the way the Gospels are."

Do you want to say anything else?

"I'm a great magician, but I'm afraid that they remember Peter the magician more than me."

MAGIC IN ANCIENT TIMES

The word "magic" was originally used to describe the acts of Persian and Chaldean magicians, who probably belonged to the priestly class and were skilled in astrology and divination.

Later on, however, magic was understood as a "science" which allowed one to control the forces of nature. It included all the strange practices that served to obtain that control.

More than a science, however, magic is a pseudo science—a false science. Magic continues to repeat the same practices, while science is animated by the spirit of research. It always attempts new experiments to test certain hypotheses and so make progress.

Some people confuse magic with religion. However, even though they both arise from similar needs, in reality they follow two very different paths. Religion maintains that the world is ruled by one or more personal supernatural beings, to whom sacrifices and prayers are directed. Magic claims that the world is ruled by impersonal forces which it's possible to control in order to change the course of events.

While the Bible strictly condemns magic, in some ancient civilizations—such as Egypt and India—magic was held in esteem. The Greeks of the classic age looked upon it with great suspicion. This attitude changed radically in the Hellenistic period, when magic—along with astrology and alchemy—began to arouse great interest. People felt that the universe was under the control of occult laws and forces whose secrets human beings could discover.

Simon the Magician was a "son" of this mentality. He created much confusion between his tricks and the miracles performed by Peter and John in the name of Jesus. He thought that the apostles were magicians, as he was. That's why it seemed normal to him to offer money so he could learn their strategies.

Barnabas, a Missionary Giant

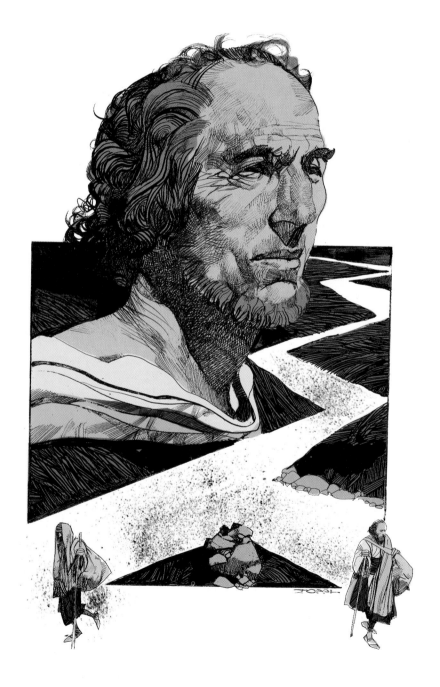

"And so it was that Joseph, a Levite born in Cyprus, whom the apostles called Barnabas (which means 'One who encourages'), sold a field he owned, brought the money, and turned it over to the apostles."
(Acts 4:36-37)

Barnabas. Is that a Hebrew name?
"Yes. It means 'one who encourages.' But my name was Joseph. A Hebrew of the tribe of Levi, I was born in Cyprus and was the cousin of Mark, the evangelist. When I converted to Christianity, the apostles gave me the name Barnabas."

You're considered a great missionary and are often given the title "apostle." Where was the first Christian missionary work carried out?
"At first, missionary work was carried out only in the holy land and in nearby districts where Hebrew colonies had sprung up. In fact, the apostles seemed to think that the announcement of the Gospel would not be made to everyone, but only to the Hebrew

people. But then Peter had a vision that changed his outlook. As a result, a whole Gentile household came into the Church. Later, after the mission undertaken by Paul and me at Antioch, the problem of the universality of Christianity was faced and resolved."

Tell me about Paul of Tarsus. What was he like?

"He had a keen intelligence, typically Hebrew in its subtleness, and a fiery personality. His first reaction to Jesus, whom he had not known personally, and to all Christians, was one of violent dislike. He considered them preachers of false teachings. When one of them, Stephen, happened to come within his reach, he enthusiastically participated in his stoning. One day, Paul—who was called Saul in those days—heard that the Christians were getting converts in Damascus and he asked the Sanhedrin to let him go there to arrest them. But during that trip he was stopped by a flash of light. He heard a voice saying, 'Saul, Saul, why do you persecute me?' 'Who are you?' Paul asked, amazed. 'I am Jesus,' came the reply. Paul was blinded for three days, then he went to have himself baptized and became the most able preacher of our faith."

Did you like Paul?

"It was somewhat difficult to get along with him. But I was the one who told the apostles that he was sincere in his conversion. I was also the one who went to look for him in Tarsus, where he had been forced to stay for some years. I brought him with me to Antioch. I've never regretted that act."

Not even when you ended your relationship with him?

"Our friendship was so genuine that there was never a definite ending. At a certain point our paths divided, as the paths of Abraham and Lot had divided over almost two thousand years before."

What was Antioch like?

"It was a magnificent city, one of the most important in the East, with more than half a million inhabitants. A huge highway cut through it that was almost a hundred feet wide. This was lined with porticoes, temples, palaces and statues. The Hebrew community there was very large. Many of its members had converted to the way of Jesus. The word 'Christians' was first used in Antioch."

What was happening in Antioch?

"The Christian community was having a wonderful experience. In fact, the word of God was being addressed not only to the Hebrews, but also to the Gentiles, who were entering the people of God without submitting to the prescriptions of the Mosaic law. The pagan converts, in fact, didn't understand why they should be circumcised. Then there was the issue of food.... I was of the opinion that the pagan converts weren't obliged to live by Jewish rules in order to become Christians."

But they didn't think the same way in Jerusalem, did they, or am I mistaken?

"A Church meeting was called in Jerusalem for this reason. It resolved the issue. It freed the Gentile converts from all but some very simple Hebrew laws."

Why was circumcision so important for the Hebrews?

"It was a law observed by Abraham. It was the sign of belonging to the people of the covenant, to Israel."

And there was also the law of the Sabbath rest. That was quite strict, wasn't it?

"Yes, there were detailed rules about an endless number of things. For example, how much weight could be transported on the Sabbath without violating the holy day? A tailor couldn't take his needle with him when he left the house; a man couldn't go out with nailed shoes on.... With the passing of time, these rules had multiplied and had altered the meaning of the religious observance. During the Sabbath it was obviously forbidden to harvest grain, but the strictest Hebrews even forbade gathering two heads of grain. And so on."

Didn't these rules create some inconveniences?

"Yes, and not just a few. During the Greek persecution two centuries before Jesus, a group of Hebrews preferred to be massacred rather than violate the Sabbath by carrying weapons to defend themselves. The Jewish people were so attached to the observance of the Sabbath rest that even the Romans respected this holy day, although they didn't understand it. Tacitus considered it a useless waste of time; the poet Juvenal attributed it to laziness. The powerful Roman Empire gave up enrolling Hebrews in their legions because it feared they would lay down their weapons the moment the Sabbath began.

"Of course, when not taken to extremes, a weekly day of rest

is beneficial to both body and spirit. The *idea* is good—in fact, it comes from Scripture—but the application got out of hand at a certain point."

Who was the first Christian missionary?
"As far as I know, a man from Gerasa, a place on the eastern shore of Lake Genneseret, whom Jesus had freed from evil spirits."

Why him instead of anyone else?
"That man begged Jesus to bring him with him. Instead, Jesus told him to go back home and tell what the goodness of God had done for him. The man went back to the city to tell what had happened to him. Jesus had wanted to leave a witness behind him, one of the first missionaries in the history of Christianity."

Barnabas, you've traveled a lot. Could you tell me about one of your experiences?
"In Lystra, Timothy's city, Paul and I were mistaken for the Greek gods Hermes (Mercury) and Zeus (Jupiter). We had to do a lot of explaining to set the people straight. And finally when they did understand that we weren't gods, some troublemakers came along and stoned Paul. He almost died."

THE ROADS OF THE HOLY LAND AND THE ROMAN EMPIRE

The holy land has always been a passageway between Syria and Egypt or Arabia, between the interior of Asia and the Mediterranean. Therefore, in Jesus' time it was crossed by caravan routes, which were followed by travelers and merchants, who almost always banded together in large groups to better defend themselves from possible attacks by robbers. They traveled mostly by walking or by riding animals, because the condition of the roads rarely permitted the use of carriages. Donkeys and camels were the animals most commonly used for transporting people and things, but at the time of Jesus, horses which previously had been used almost exclusively in war, were becoming more common as a means of transportation.

Under the dominion of Rome, the holy land also made a noticeable improvement in its highway system. The Romans were masters of road construction. To allow for a rapid transfer of their troops, they built a colossal road network that connected Rome to all the provinces of the empire. These roads were well-paved with stones and very practical even in the rain. They spanned brooks, rivers, marshes and mountains, with bridges, embankments and tunnels that were admirable examples of engineering.

It has been calculated that in their whole empire, the Romans constructed more than 50,000 miles of roads. To a large degree this fact favored the spread of Christianity, for the roads were traveled not only by soldiers, imperial messengers and merchants, but also by the apostles and other Christian missionaries. Within a few years these missionaries brought the "good news" to the boundaries of the then-known world.

But he survived, didn't he? Any other episodes?

"In the course of our travels we arrived at Paphos, the capital of the island of Cyprus. The Roman governor resided there. His name was Sergius Paulus and his title was proconsul. He was a wise person, very curious and interested in eastern religions. Sergius Paulus wanted to meet us, and he wanted to know which faith we were preaching. Among the proconsul's retinue there was a Jewish magician who called himself Bar-Jesus. He was opposed to this meeting. Looking him in the eye, Paul said to him, 'You will be blind and you won't see the sun for a little while.' Immediately that 'magician' lost his sight."

Where were the first Christian communities established?

"After Jesus' death, the first Christian community was formed in Jerusalem. From there the apostles and the disciples went out to preach. The greatest number of 'churches' sprang up in Antioch, which for some years was the center of the missionary activity of the Church. There were churches in Cyprus, my homeland; in Philippi; in Thrace; in Corinth, which at the time was considered the capital of vice.... Among the most an-cient Christian communities were those in Alexandria, Thessalonica, Ephesus and Carthage."

And what about Rome?

"After Antioch, Rome became the center of Christianity. Eventually Peter settled there. It was in Rome that Peter would suffer martyrdom."

Did Paul visit all these communities?

"He was the one who founded most of them. Paul traveled a lot, more than anyone else. He may even have gone as far as Spain."

Paul wrote much, I know. Did you write something, too?

"They attribute to me a Gospel that was lost and an epistle that bears my name. That letter attacks those who would like to force the Gentile converts to observe Hebrew laws."

Where did you die?

"In my homeland, Cyprus. According to tradition, I was martyred in Salamis, a city on the island's east coast."

Paul, the Apostle of the Gentiles

"As Saul was coming near the city of Damascus, suddenly a light from the sky flashed around him. He fell to the ground and heard a voice saying to him, 'Saul, Saul! Why do you persecute me?' 'Who are you, Lord?' he asked. 'I am Jesus whom you persecute,' the voice said."
(Acts 9:3-5)

Would you like to introduce yourself?
"I'm of the Hebrew race and a Roman citizen. I was born in Tarsus in Cilicia, which was a Roman province. My father was a well-to-do Pharisee, of middle-class origin. He gave me something very precious, at least for that time—Roman citizenship."

Is your name Saul or Paul?
"I took the Roman name Paul when I began to preach to the 'Gentiles,' that is, the non-Hebrews. Saul is my Hebrew name. Those of us Hebrews who lived outside the holy land usually had two names."

Were you a child-wonder?
"I would say, rather, an obstinate child."

Did you know Jesus personally?
"I was a few years younger

than he, and I never met him while he was alive and preaching. I met him in an extraordinary way on the road that led to Damascus."

Were you a persecutor of the Christians?

"Yes, I was a bitter enemy of the new religion. For me, a strict Pharisee, it was a serious threat to the religion of Moses. The leaders of the Sanhedrin in Jerusalem had entrusted me with the responsibility of annihilating the Christians in Damascus."

And what happened?

"I saw Jesus risen and alive. He blinded me and I fell to the ground. Then he asked this question that changed my life: 'Why do you persecute me?' It jolted me. I had been persecuting the Christians, not Jesus, I thought. Then I understood that Jesus was present in every Christian."

Sometimes you're called the founder of Christianity. Is that true?

"No. I only said that the message and the salvation that Jesus brought were addressed to all people."

And what about that public encounter with Peter, the head of the apostles, in Antioch?

"It enabled us to let down the barriers between the Hebrews and the Gentiles. While staying loyal to Peter, I made a clarification. He, too, believed in the universality of Christ's message. He also knew that if we followed those who didn't want to break away from Hebrew traditions, Christianity would become just a Hebrew heresy. It would end there."

Who was the person you loved the most?

"Before I met Jesus, it was Gamaliel, my master in Jerusalem. He had the knowledge and wisdom of a patriarch. I also loved very much a young man from Troas whom I brought back to life in the name of Christ. His name was Eutychus. He had fallen asleep during one of my sermons (it must have been boring) and had died after falling from the third floor. What a desperate moment for his parents and for me!"

Why were you so fond of Gamaliel?

"He was an exceptional man. I'll tell you about just one episode. When the apostles were arrested in Jerusalem, some members of the Sanhedrin wanted them to be sentenced to death. Gamaliel advised using caution. He wisely said, 'Leave them alone! If what they have planned and done is of human origin, it will disappear, but if it comes from God, you cannot possibly defeat them.'"

You're not one of the "Twelve." Why did they give you the title "apostle"?

"Because of the great extent and importance of my missionary work. The title 'apostle' was also rightly given to my friend Barnabas."

On a map we can see the complicated routes of your travels

and have an idea of the greatness of your missionary achievements. How many miles did you cover?

"An enormous number. I crossed oceans, I went through mountain passes, I traveled to inaccessible places. They tried to stone me once, when I had been mistaken for Hermes, the Greek god. I escaped from Damascus by being lowered in a basket from a window in the city wall. I faced difficulties and hostility. In Philippi I was beaten and put in prison, in Corinth I was dragged into court in front of the proconsul Gallio, brother of the philosopher Seneca. In Athens they ridiculed me. Everywhere, however, I brought people into the Christian faith and started Christian communities."

Could you tell me about an episode in your travels?

"During my third journey, which lasted four years, I settled in the great commercial city of Ephesus. One day there was a great uproar brought on by merchants who sold souvenirs. Conversions to Christianity had interfered with the sales of statues of the goddess Diana and other pagan souvenirs. A riot threatened to break out. Fortunately, the city clerk calmed the merchants, but I decided it was time to move on."

SEA VOYAGES

In Biblical times, Israel was never a sea-faring people, even though from its early years it had contacts with great nations of sea traders, like the Phoenicians and the Egyptians. In the tenth century B.C., with the help of the Phoenicians, King Solomon succeeded in creating a merchant fleet for transporting goods and raw materials up and down the Red Sea. This experience, however, is a practically isolated episode in the long history of the Hebrew people, even though they owned a long stretch of land along the Mediterranean. A possible explanation for this is the shortage of good harbors in biblical times.

In Jesus' day, the Mediterranean was completely under Rome's control. In order to protect its ships traveling between Italy and the provinces of the empire, Rome fought piracy with great determination.

Nevertheless, the ships of that era weren't able to navigate in the open sea all year round. The Mediterranean could be crossed without too many risks only during the period from April to October. During winter, ships didn't venture out to sea, or else they traveled along the coast in brief stages.

A great traveler both by land and by sea was the apostle Paul. It seems that he crossed parts of the whole Mediterranean basin as far as the Iberian Peninsula. Four of his journeys are definitely known. On the first one, he left Antioch in Syria, disembarked in Cyprus, crossed the island, took to sea again and stopped in Lycia. Then he traveled through Pamphylia, Pisidia and Galatia, went back to Lycia and returned by sea to Antioch.

On his second journey, he left Antioch, crossed all of Asia Minor, and sailed over to Macedonia and Greece. Then he sailed to Caesarea, after a brief stopover in Asia Minor, and returned by land to Antioch in Syria. The main cities he had visited were Derbe, Lystra, Iconium, Antioch in Pisidia, Troas, Philippi, Thessalonica, Beroea, Athens, Corinth and Ephesus.

He took a similar route on his third journey. He left Antioch in Syria and stayed for more than two years in Ephesus. Then he went on to Troas, Philippi and Corinth, back to Philippi and Troas, then to Miletus, Rhodes, Tyre, Caesarea and finally Jerusalem.

Paul made his fourth journey as a prisoner, when he was sent to Rome for trial. From Caesarea he went to Sidon, to Myra in Lycia and to the island of Crete. He was shipwrecked on Malta, but all the ship's passengers and crew were saved. After taking to the sea again, he went to Syracuse, Reggio Calabria and Puteoli. From there he traveled by land to Rome.

Why are you called "apostle of the Gentiles"?

"Because I brought Jesus' message to the various peoples of the Greek and Roman world. I helped to separate Christianity from connections with Judaism, because these were hindering its spread. At the same time, though, I always tried first—in every town or city—to convert my fellow Hebrews, but my attempts in this area were usually unsuccessful."

You arrived in Rome as a prisoner. How did they treat you?

"The Romans listened to me patiently because I held Roman citizenship, but they didn't understand what I was talking about. The only thing they understood was that politics had nothing to do with my imprisonment. They treated me well. They assigned a soldier to keep me under house arrest, but they let me choose my home. Members of the Jewish and Judeo-Christian colonies came to visit me. But the Hebrew leaders rejected with horror the idea that baptism was more important than circumcision."

How many Hebrews resided in Rome?

"I think more than 40,000 out of a million inhabitants. Their social conditions were modest. Many of them were former prisoners from the holy land or slaves. But the Jewish slaves who were faithful to their religion, refused to work on the Sabbath and to eat food that wasn't ritually prepared. Therefore, they were less useful than others, and usually their Roman owners ended up freeing them or letting them be redeemed by someone of the same religion. The Roman intellectuals were strongly anti-Hebrew. Soon this aversion was also directed at the Christians, who were considered a Jewish sect."

There were many slaves in Rome. What did Christianity do for them?

"Christianity immediately showed that it had something to say to them, too. In fact, Jesus had proclaimed the dignity of every human person. I had faced the problem of slavery before when I was in Asia Minor. I had advised the masters to treat their slaves well and the slaves not to cheat their masters. Little by little, of course, Christianity helped to eliminate slavery in one part of the world after another."

Even today your letters form the basis of theology, the study of everything related to God. How many did you write?

"Many, but not all have been preserved. On the other hand, although there are thirteen in the New Testament that are attributed to me, some of these were actually written by my disciples, presenting my key thoughts in their own ways. The letters I directly wrote or dictated were to the people of Rome, Corinth, Galatia, Philippi and Thessalonica. I also wrote a letter to a dear friend, Philemon."

What do you mean by the phrase, "Those who don't work, don't eat!?"

"The exact phrase is, 'Whoever refuses to work is not allowed to eat.' It was a common proverb among the Hebrews and also among the wise men of paganism. I repeated it to the Thessalonians who, believing that Christ's return and the end of the world were close, had stopped working and were living off the work of others."

Why didn't you do anything to save yourself from Nero's persecution?

"I didn't look for martyrdom, but I accepted it. I died by being beheaded, like John the Baptist."

Timothy, Paul's Beloved Disciple

"Paul traveled on to Derbe and Lystra, where a Christian named Timothy lived. His mother, who was also a Christian, was Jewish, but his father was a Greek. All the believers in Lystra and Iconium spoke well of Timothy. Paul wanted to take Timothy along with him, so he circumcised him. He did so because all the Hebrews who lived in those places knew that Timothy's father was Greek."
(Acts 16:1-3)

What was Paul to you?
"He was my teacher, my father and even my doctor. I was delicate and my health was frail. Once, he advised me to drink not only water, but to mix a little wine with it to help my stomach."

When did you meet him for the first time?
"During his first missionary journey, Paul had stopped in my small city of Lystra in

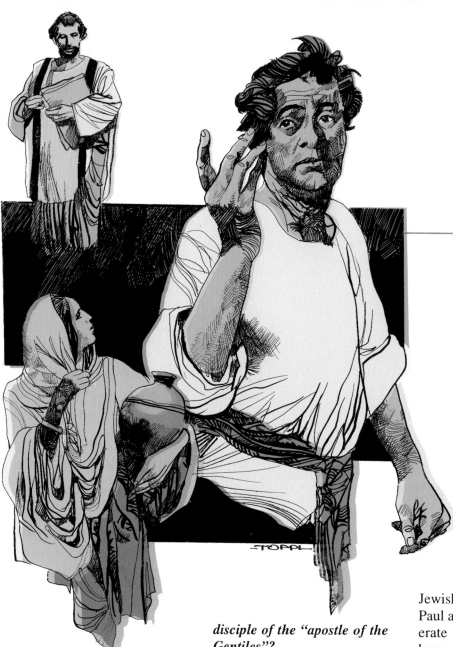

Lycaonia, in Asia Minor. Barnabas was with him."

And Paul chose you as his collaborator?

"Not immediately. Two or three years later Paul returned to Lystra, where in the meantime a small Christian community had been organized. That was when I became his disciple."

How did an unlearned person like you become the beloved
disciple of the "apostle of the Gentiles"?

"I wasn't really unlearned. My father was a pagan, but my mother Eunice and my grandmother Lois were of Hebrew origin. They had educated me in the fear of God and love for his word. I knew perfectly the history of the people of Israel, the story of Moses and the law. But out of respect for my father, who was Greek, my mother hadn't had me circumcised."

So Paul had you circumcised. Why?

"It was out of respect for the
Jewish people of that region. Paul always tried to be considerate toward his fellow Hebrews. In fact, in any 'new' town or city, he always preached first in the synagogue."

And after that you accompanied Paul?

"Yes, sharing the troubles and the opposition. I was his spokesman on several occasions, until I became the head of the Church in Ephesus."

Is it true that there were some Christians in Ephesus who believed in different doctrines?

"They were followers of John

the Baptist. John's violent death hadn't put an end to his movement. I don't know how they ended up in Ephesus. Maybe they had escaped from Galilee to avoid the persecution of Herod Antipas. They were unaware that there was a baptism in the name of the Lord Jesus. Their baptism was John the Baptist's, one of purification and penitence, not of salvation. Paul instructed them, though, and then they received Christian baptism."

Did you travel a lot?
"I traveled quite a bit in Macedonia and Greece with Paul and also alone, when Paul had decided that I was capable and mature. I went to Philippi, Thessalonica and Beroea. I stayed for years in Corinth and Ephesus...."

What was Corinth like?
"There were many temples dedicated to the Greek gods. Corinth was an important trading center where vice and corruption reigned. There were sailors, merchants and adventurers."

Did any strange episodes take place during your many travels?
"A very memorable one happened in Philippi, a city in Macedonia. I was with Paul

THE ORIGIN OF THE NAME "CHRISTIAN"

The *Acts of the Apostles* (11:26) tells us: "It was at Antioch that believers were first called *Christians*." It's not specified who coined this name, which began to distinguish Jesus Christ's followers. Probably the pagans invented it. The Christians called each other *brothers, disciples, saints, faithful ones* and *chosen ones*, while the Judeans called them *Galileans, Nazarenes* or even *heretics* (persons who had adopted false beliefs).

Antioch was the capital of the province of Syria and the third largest city of the Roman Empire. It was the place of refuge for many Christians who had escaped from Jerusalem because of the persecutions that broke out after the death of Stephen. Christians found a favorable atmosphere in the Syrian capital. New converts were made and one of the most important original Christian communities was formed. The group became so large that it could not go unnoticed by the pagan inhabitants. These looked for a name to give these people, many of whom had been pagans themselves but now professed a new religion. The name "Christians" was invented. In the beginning it probably contained a hint of contempt. In fact, more than fifty years passed before this word was adopted by the Christians themselves.

Even the first references by Latin writers to Jesus and to Christians contain negative judgments. Tacitus tells that the common people hated the followers of the new religion and called them *chrestiani* (it should be noted that in Greek *chrestòs* means "good," but also "foolish"). Very soon, however, those who understood the true nature of Christianity became more and more numerous. People began to join the new religion. Despite the persecutions, in less than three centuries almost the whole Roman Empire had become Christian.

and Silas. Luke was with us, too. Yes, the same Luke who wrote a Gospel and the *Acts of the Apostles*. Every day we were followed by a slave girl who was considered to be a fortune teller. She had moments when she acted like someone possessed by the devil. Finally, Paul confronted

her. Addressing the spirit that had taken possession of her, he said, 'In the name of Jesus Christ I order you to come out of her!' The slave girl was cured at once, but she lost the ability to predict the future. This aroused the resentment of her masters. They had made their living off her by getting

paid for the 'predictions' she uttered during her outbursts. Paul and Silas were brought before the officials of the city and sentenced to jail for disturbing public order. They were also beaten. But soon everything was cleared up. After spending a night in chains, they were released."

What was the question that people asked you the most?
"What do I have to do to be saved?"

And what was your answer?
"Believe in the Lord Jesus and you'll be saved, together with your family."

Have you also been to Rome?
"I went there to say farewell to Paul when he was about to die, but I didn't stay for very long. He himself advised me to return to Ephesus."

In your time, what sacraments were celebrated?
"At the beginning of Christianity, two sacraments in particular were administered: baptism and confirmation. They weren't separated as they are today, because baptism was given to people who were adult converts. Naturally, there was also the ordination of priests, who were called presbyters. And there was the anointing of the sick. And finally, on the 'day of the Lord,' which corresponded to your Sunday, the community celebrated the Eucharist."

But wasn't the Sabbath your holy day?
"It still is for the Hebrews, even in your time. For the early Christians, though, Sunday was substituted for the strict celebration of the Sabbath, in honor of the resurrection of Jesus."

What about marriage?
"It was civil. From a religious point of view, the matrimonial union was blessed by the priests. On the other hand, great attention was given to funerals. When a person died, everything had to be prepared for his or her resurrection. The body had to have its tomb. The priests officiated during the burial. The tombs were often constructed according to the Syrian and Etruscan custom, in crypts dug out of the walls of long underground tunnels, which were called catacombs."

But weren't catacombs the hiding places of the Christians?
"That happened only during the last persecutions. Catacombs were Christian cemeteries up until the ninth century, then this custom went into decline. They were covered over and forgotten. They began to be rediscovered in the sixteenth century. The fact that their tunnels were complicated and twisted, a real underground spider's web, made people think they had been constructed as Christian hiding places. Many novels have been based on this hypothesis."

Who is the most appealing Old Testament figure for you?
"Jonah, the prophet who disobeyed God and then went to preach in the corrupt city of Nineveh."

What does friendship mean to you?
"It's the most noble sentiment, along with love, necessary for living as a human being."

How long did you live?
"A person's life is not measured by how many years he or she has lived."

Did you die a martyr, as tradition implies?
"I died happy that I had helped to spread the word of the Lord Jesus."

APPENDIX

New Testament Personalities

Agabus

A prophet of Jerusalem who predicted to the Christians of Antioch that there would be a severe famine in Judea. He also predicted that Paul would be arrested if he went to Jerusalem *(Acts 11:27-28; 21:10-11).*

Agrippa

(See Herod.)

Alexander

1) A Son of Simon of Cyrene, the man who carried Jesus' cross to Calvary *(Mark 15:21).*
2) A priest and member of the Sanhedrin, who, along with other Hebrews, interrogated the apostles *(Acts 4:6).*
3) A Hebrew who tried to speak to the mob in Ephesus during the uproar caused by the silver-smiths *(Acts 19:33).*
4) An apostate who was expelled from the Christian community by Paul *(1 Timothy 1:20).*
5) A coppersmith who was an adversary of Paul *(2 Timothy 4:14).*

Ananias

1) A Christian who was struck dead for having lied to the Apostle Peter *(Acts 5:1).*
2) A Christian who lived in Damascus. Jesus told him to go to a certain house, where he would find Paul, who had been there for three days and was completely blind. Ananias restored Paul's sight *(Acts 9:10-19).*
3) A high priest present at Paul's questioning by the Sanhedrin. He ordered his assistants to beat Paul. When Paul was tried by Felix, the Roman governor of Cesarea, Ananias became his accuser *(Acts 23:1-5; 24:1).*

Andrew

One of the first apostles chosen by Jesus. A fisher-man from Bethsaida, on the lake of Galilee, he was the brother of Simon Peter. According to tradition, he was crucified in Patras on a cross in the shape of an X, which became known as "the cross of St Andrew" *(John 1:35-42; 6:6; 12:20-22; Matthew 4:18-20; 10:2; Acts 1:13).*

Anna

An elderly prophetess who was present at the temple of Jerusalem when Joseph and Mary brought the infant Jesus to consecrate him to God. She recognized Jesus as the Messiah *(Luke 2:36-38).*

Annas

The high priest from A.D. 6 to 15. Together with his son-in-law Caiaphas, he presided over the assembly that interrogated Jesus *(Luke 3:2; John 18:12-13).*

Antipas

(See Herod.)

Apollos

A Hebrew preacher from Alexandria, who became an eloquent Christian speaker. He was active in the communities in Ephesus and Corinth *(Acts 18:24-19:1; 1 Corinthians 1:11-13; 3:5-9, 21-23; 16:12).*

Aquila

A Judeo-Christian and friend of Paul. He had to leave Italy with his wife Priscilla when the emperor Claudius expelled the Hebrews from Rome in A.D. 48. He was a tentmaker, and Paul worked with him for a time in Corinth. Aquila and Priscilla followed Paul to Ephesus and later returned to Rome. Christians gathered in their home for prayer *(Acts 18:1-3, 26; Romans 3-5; 1 Corinthians 16:19; 2 Timothy 4:19).*

Archelaus

(See Herod.)

Aretas

The fourth king of that name to reign in Arabia Petrea, today called Jordan (9 B.C.-A.D. 40). One of his daughters married Herod Antipas, who later put her aside and married Herodias. Offended by the treatment of his daughter, Aretas declared war on Antipas and defeated him. A governor under Aretas in Damascus tried to arrest Paul, but the apostle managed to escape by being lowered from the wall in a huge trading basket *(2 Corinthians 11:32).*

Aristarchus

A Macedonian Christian, friend and collaborator of Paul. He followed Paul to Ephesus, to Jerusalem and to Rome. He was close to Paul during his imprisonment *(Acts 19:29; 20:4; 27:2; Colossians 4:10).*

Barabbas

A Hebrew robber, murderer and revolutionary detained in Jerusalem when Jesus was arrested. The Roman procurator, Pilate, was convinced of Jesus' innocence. He tried to save Jesus by making use of the right that permitted him to free one condemned man on the celebration of the Passover. He asked the crowd to choose between Jesus and Barabbas, and they chose Barabbas, who was then freed *(Matthew 27:15-26).*

Barnabas

A Levite born in Cyprus, and an important collaborator of the apostles. He was called Joseph, and when he converted, the apostles gave him the name Barnabas, which means "son of consolation or encouragement." Together with Paul, he evangelized the Gentiles in Cyprus and Asia Minor.

Tradition says he was martyred in Cyprus. In the *Acts of the Apostles*, Barnabas, along with the Twelve and Paul, is called an "apostle" *(Acts 4:36-37; 9:27; 11:22-26; 12:25-15:39; 1 Corinthians 9:6; Galatians 2:1-14).*

Bartholomew

One of the twelve apostles, of whom we know very little. His name is found in the list of the apostles in the first three Gospels, while John puts the name "Nathanael" in its place; they are most likely the same person. Jesus calls him a "true Israelite." We do not know exactly where he preached. A legend says that he was skinned alive and crucified in Armenia. His body is said to have been brought to Rome and placed in the sanctuary dedicated to him on the island Tiberina *(Matthew 10:3; Acts 1:13).*

Bartimaeus

A blind beggar from Jericho, cured by Jesus *(Mark 10:46-52).*

Bernice

The sister of Herod Agrippa II; she went to live with her brother when she was widowed by Herod of Chalcis. She then married Polemon, the king of Cilicia, but it was a short-lived marriage. Bernice then went back to live with her brother *(Acts 25-26).*

Caesar

The title of the Roman emperor at the time of the New Testament. When Jesus was born, Caesar Augustus was reigning, and his successor was Tiberius Caesar. Peter and Paul died as martyrs under Nero. Jesus sometimes used the term Caesar to mean "the power of the government" *(Mark 12:14-17; Luke 2:1; 3:1; Acts 25:8-12).*

Caiaphas

The high priest of Jerusalem (18-36 A.D.). He presided over the assembly that condemned Jesus and was a relentless persecutor of the Christians until the Roman governor of Syria, Vitellius, relieved him of his duty as high priest. It is not known how he died *(Matthew 26:3; Luke 3:2; John 11:45-53; 18:13-14; Acts 5:17).*

Claudius

The fourth Roman emperor (A.D. 41-54). He made the Hebrews leave Rome *(Acts 11:28).*

Claudius Lysias

The commander of the Roman garrison in Jerusalem. He saved Paul from a ferocious mob of his fellow countrymen. To protect Paul from being assassinated, Lysias sent him to Caesarea, so that he could be tried by the Roman governor, Felix *(Acts 21:31-23:30).*

Clement

A Christian of Philippi and a collaborator of Paul *(Philippians 4:3)*.

Cleophas

One of the two travelers to Emmaus, who met the risen Jesus *(Luke 24:13-35)*.

Cornelius

A Roman Centurion stationed at Caesarea. An angel came to him in a dream and told him to send for Peter, whom he would find in Joppa. At Cornelius' house, Peter found the family and a group of friends of the Roman official. They were the first group of non-Hebrews to be converted to Christianity *(Acts 10)*.

Crescens

A friend of Paul's who was close to him during his imprisonment in Rome; later, he went to preach in Galatia *(2 Timothy 4:10)*.

Crispus

The head of the Jewish synagogue in Corinth. Paul converted him and his family *(Acts 18:8; 1 Corinthians 1:14)*.

Demas

One of Paul's collaborators in Rome. He later abandoned Paul and went to Thessalonica *(Colossians 4:14; 2 Timothy 4:10)*.

Demetrius

A jeweler from Ephesus who organized the demonstration of the silversmiths against Paul. In Ephesus the worship of Diana was active. After Paul preached there was a decline in the sale of souvenirs dedicated to the Greek goddess *(Acts 19:24)*.

Dionysius

A judge of the Areopagus, a tribunal of Athens. He was converted by Paul. He is said to have become the first bishop of Athens *(Acts 17:34)*.

Diotrephes

An arrogant church leader who refused to accept the authority of John *(3 John 9-10)*.

Dorcas-Tabitha

A Christian from Joppa who dedicated herself to the poor. She was brought back to life by Peter *(Acts 9:36-42)*.

Drusilla

A Hebrew princess, the wife of the Roman procurator, Felix, who concerned himself with Paul's case. She was the sister of Bernice and Agrippa II *(Acts 24:24)*.

Elizabeth

The wife of the priest Zechariah and mother of John the Baptist. She was a relative of Mary, the mother of Jesus. Her son was born when she was very old *(Luke 1:5-25, 39-80)*.

Elymas Bar-Jesus

A Jewish magician who claimed to be a prophet in the court of Sergius-Paulus, the Roman proconsul of Cyprus. He tried to stop a meeting that the proconsul wanted to have with Paul and Barnabas. To punish him, Paul made him blind for a few days *(Acts 13:6-12)*.

Epaphras

A Christian who founded the church community in Colossae. He visited Paul in prison and brought him news about the Christians of Colossae *(Colossians 1:7; 4:12-13; Philemon 2:3)*.

Epaphroditus

A messenger sent by the Philippian Church to bring a gift to Paul, who was in prison *(Philippians 2:25-30; 4:18)*.

Erastus

1) One of Paul's helpers. He went to preach in Macedonia with Timothy while Paul stayed in Asia Minor *(Acts 19:22; 2 Timothy 4:20)*.
2) A treasurer from Corinth. He was a Christian and sent his greetings to the Christians of Rome *(Romans 16:23)*.

Eunice

The mother of Timothy. She had married a pagan from Lystra, but she educated her son to respect the laws of Moses *(Acts 16:1; 2 Timothy 1:5)*.

Eutychus

A young man who came to listen to Paul in Troas. He fell asleep, fell out the window, and died. Paul brought him back to life *(Acts 20:7-12)*.

Felix

A Roman governor in Caesarea, to whom Paul was brought to be tried. He kept the apostle in prison for two years, in the hope that he would receive a bribe for Paul's release *(Acts 23:23-24:27)*.

Festus

The Roman governor at Caesarea, after Felix. He called Paul to defend himself before King Agrippa II and Bernice *(Acts 24:27-26:32)*.

Gabriel

The archangel, a special messenger of God, who was sent to announce the birth of John the Baptist to Zechariah and the birth of Jesus to Mary *(Luke 1:5-38)*.

Gaius

1) A Macedonian Christian who was with Paul during his third missionary journey. He was dragged to the amphitheater during the demonstration of the jewelers in Ephesus *(Acts 19:29)*.
2) A Christian from Derbe. He accompanied Paul to Jerusalem *(Acts 20:4)*.
3) One of the few Christians baptized by Paul in Corinth *(1 Corinthians 1:14)*.
4) A Christian friend to whom John addressed his third letter *(3 John 1)*.

Gallio

The Roman proconsul of Achaia between A.D. 51 and 53, tutor to the emperor Nero, and brother of the philosopher, Seneca. When he was the governor of Achaia, he lived in Corinth. Worried about Paul's preaching in Corinth, some Jewish leaders tried to convince Gallio to imprison the apostle. Instead, he dismissed them because he didn't want to get involved in religious matters *(Acts 18:12-17)*.

Gamaliel

A well known Pharisee and member of the Sanhedrin, the supreme Hebrew council. He was Paul's teacher. When the apostles were brought before the Sanhedrin for the second time, Gamaliel intervened and advised their release *(Acts 5:34-39; 22:3)*.

Herod

The name of an Idumean family who exercised control in Judea from the middle of the first century B.C. to A.D. 93. Herod is not a Hebrew name: it's Greek and it means "belonging to a class of heroes."

1) Herod the Great: Son of Antipater. The Romans gave him the title "King of the Jews." He reigned from 37 B.C. to 4 B.C. He was an excellent administator and a tireless constructor. He built the temple of Jerusalem, the Fortress Antonia, and the royal palace west of the city. He reconstructed the city of Samaria, renaming it Sebaste (the Greek name for Augustus,) and he created an artificial port which he named Cesarea. But he never managed to be loved by the people. He was known for his serious crimes. The Gospel reminds us of the slaughter of innocent children in Bethlehem. Herod also had everyone killed who opposed him, including forty-five members of the Sanhedrin. He did away with his wife Mariamne, his mother-in-law, and two of his sons. He divided his kingdom between his sons Archelaus, Antipas, and Philip *(Matthew 2:1-20; Luke 1:5)*.

2) Archelaus: Son of Herod the Great. Named Herod the Ethnarc, he governed Judea from 4 B.C. to A.D. 6. He too was a ruthless dictator; he treated the Judeans and the Samaritans so cruelly that the Romans dismissed him and sent him into exile *(Matthew 2:22)*.

3) Antipas: Another son of Herod the Great. Named Herod the Tetrarch, he governed Galilee from 4 B.C. to A.D. 39. He had John the Baptist beheaded. Pilate sent Jesus to him to be tried, since Jesus came from Galilee. Antipas refused to judge Jesus and sent him back to Pilate *(Matthew 14:1-12; Mark 6:14-29; Luke 3:19-20; 9:7-9; 23:6-16)*.

4) Agrippa I: Called King Herod, the son of Aristobulus, and the grandson of Herod the Great. He governed Galilee, Judea and Samaria until A.D. 44. To gain the favor of the people, he persecuted the Christians. He had the Apostle James, son of Zebedee, beheaded, and he imprisoned Peter *(Acts 12:1-4; 19-23)*.

5) Agrippa II: Son of Agrippa I. When he was in Caesarea visiting the governor, he was presented with Paul's case. His verdict was that Paul could have been released if he hadn't appealed to Caesar. In A.D. 66, Agrippa tried to convince the people of Jerusalem to give up the rebellion against Rome. In A.D. 70, at Caesarea Philippi, he celebrated with Titus the victory over the Judean rebels *(Acts 25:13-26:32)*.

Herodias

A Hebrew princess (7 B.C. to A.D. 39). She was the wife of Philip and scandalized the Hebrews because she left her husband to live with Herod Antipas (Philip's half-brother). Disturbed because John the Baptist reminded Herod that they were living in sin, Herodias made use of the charms of her daughter Salome to have the Baptist killed *(Matthew 14:1-12; Mark 6:14-29; Luke 3:19)*.

Hymenaeus

A former Christian who was expelled from the Christian community by Paul because he disturbed the faith of believers with false doctrine *(1 Timothy 1:20)*.

Jairus

The head of the synagogue at Capernaum. He asked Jesus to heal his twelve-year-old daughter. Even though she was already dead by the time Jesus arrived, Jesus brought her back to life *(Mark 5:22-43)*.

James

1) Called "the greater" or "elder," a son of Zebedee and brother of John. He was a fisherman and one of the first disciples to be called by Jesus, along with his brother John. They were both nicknamed "Boanerges," which means "sons of thunder," because their straightforward and open personalities. After the ascension of Jesus, the Apostle James is said to have preached in Judea and Samaria. Then according to legend, he went to preach in Spain. After returning to Jerusalem, he was imprisoned by Herod Agrippa, who had him beheaded in A.D. 44. James was the first apostle to die a martyr's death *(Matthew 4:21-22; 10:2; 17:1-13; 26:36-46; Mark 5:37-43; 10:35-45; Acts 12:2)*.

2) Called "the younger (the less)," another apostle, the son of Alpheus *(Matthew 10:3; Mark 15:40; Acts 1:13).*

3) The "brother" (cousin) of Jesus. He was the head of the Church of Jerusalem and probably wrote the letter of James. According to some people, James "the younger" and this James ("the Just") are the same person. The Hebrew historian Flavius Josephus says that James the Just was stoned to death in A.D. 62 *(1 Corinthians 15:7; James; Matthew 13:55; Acts 12:17; 15:13-21; Galatians 2:9, 12).*

Jason

1) A Christian who hosted Paul and Silas in Thessalonica *(Acts 17:5).*

2) A Judeo-Christian mentioned by Paul *(Romans 16:21).*

Jesus

The Son of God, the Messiah foretold by the prophets of the Old Testament. He was born in Bethlehem a few years before the beginning of the Christian era and died on the cross in the year A.D. 30. His life and his doctrine are presented in the Gospels. Jesus, who began to preach around the age of thirty, did not present himself as the founder of a new religion. He brought to fulfillment the laws of Moses and did not announce a material kingdom, but rather, a spiritual one. Together with the twelve apostles, he taught the new law of love. One of his apostles, Judas, betrayed him. After having celebrated the Jewish Passover, and having initiated the Eucharist, Jesus was arrested and brought before the high priest Caiaphas and then before the Roman procurator, Pontius Pilate. Condemned by the first and abandoned by the second, he was crucified on Calvary between two thieves. Jesus was buried in a tomb dug out of the rock, and rose from the dead on the third day. About forty days later, he ascended into heaven, promising to be with the apostles and their followers as they began to spread his teachings throughout the world. In this way Christianity began. *(The entire New Testament refers directly or indirectly to Jesus.)*

Joanna

The wife of an official of Herod Antipas, healed by Jesus. She was part of the group of women who took care of Jesus and the twelve apostles during their journeys. She was one of the women who found the tomb empty on the day of Jesus' resurrection *(Luke 8:1; 24:10).*

John

A fisherman like his brother James and his father Zebedee. He became the apostle whom "Jesus loved." He is said to have written the *Book of Revelation.* The fourth Gospel and three letters are also attributed to him. According to tradition, he died in Ephesus at the age of 100 *(Matthew 4:20-22; 10:2; 17:1-13; Mark 3:17; 5:37-43; 10:35-45; 14:32-42; Luke 9:49-50; John 19:25-27; 20:1-10; 21:20-25; Acts 1:13; 3:3; 4:1-21; Galatians 2:9).*

John the Baptist

Called "the precursor"; the son of Zechariah and Elizabeth. He baptized Jesus in the Jordan River and called him "the lamb of God." He was beheaded at the order of Herod Antipas *(Luke 1:5-25; 44, 57-80; 3:1-22; 7:18-35; Matthew 3:1-17; 11:2-19; 14:3-12; Mark 1:2-11; 6:14-29; John 1:6-8; 15-36; 3:22-30; Acts 19:3-4).*

Joseph

Mary's husband and legal father of Jesus. Three times he received the visit of an angel sent by God: when he was told that the son of Mary was from the Holy Spirit; when he was warned that Herod wanted to kill Jesus; and when Herod died. Joseph lived in Nazareth, where he worked as a carpenter. He may have died when Jesus was still young *(Matthew 1:16-2:23; Luke 1:27; 2:1-7, 15-52).*

Joseph of Arimathea

A member of the Sanhedrin and a secret disciple of Jesus. He offered his own new tomb for Jesus to be buried in *(Luke 23:50-56; John 19:38-42).*

Judas Iscariot

The apostle who betrayed Jesus, selling him to the Sanhedrin for thirty pieces of silver. It is generally believed that the remorse he felt led him to hang himself. His name has become synonymous with traitor *(Matthew 10:4; 26:14-16, 20-25, 47-50;* 27:3-10; John 6:70-71; 12:4-8; 13:21-30; 18:2; Acts 1:16-20).*

Jude

One of the twelve apostles, called Thaddeus (generous). According to tradition, he preached in Judea, Samaria, Idumea, Syria, and Mesopotamia *(Luke 6:16; Acts 1:13).*

Julius

Roman Centurion who had custody of Paul during his voyage to Rome *(Acts 27:1).*

Lazarus

1) The brother of Mary and Martha and friend of Jesus. Jesus often visited the three of them in Bethany when going to or from Jerusalem. In the Gospel John tells of Lazarus' being raised to life by Jesus *(John 11:1-44; 12:1-11, 17-18).*
2) The name of a beggar in a famous story told by Jesus *(Luke 16:19-31).*

Luke

One of the four evangelists, probably born in Antioch of Syria. He was a physician, a companion of Paul, and author of the third Gospel and the *Acts of the Apostles.* According to tradition he was also a painter *(Colossians 4:14; 2 Timothy 4:11; Philemon 24).*

Lydia

A dye merchant who converted to Christianity after listening to the preaching of Paul to the Philippians *(Acts 16:14-15).*

Malchus

A servant of the high priest. Peter cut off his ear with a sword at the time of Jesus' arrest in the garden of Gethsemane. Jesus healed the ear and rebuked Peter *(John 18:10; Luke 22:51).*

Mark

The author of the second Gospel. Tradition identifies him with the John Mark whose mother gave hospitality to the first Christian meetings in Jerusalem. He set out with Paul and Barnabas on their first missionary journey. He left them after a while, however, and returned to Jerusalem. This bothered Paul, and he refused to take Mark on his second trip. Later on, when they were together in Rome, Mark became Paul's faithful friend and helper. Peter remembers him as "my son Mark." According to tradition, Peter provided Mark with most of the information he recorded in the second Gospel *(Acts 12:12, 25; 13:13; 15:37-39 Colossians 4:10; 2 Timothy 4:11; Philemon 24; 1 Peter 5:13).*

Martha

The sister of Mary and Lazarus. She lived in Bethany, a village near Jerusalem *(Luke 10:38-42; John 11:1-44; 12:1-2).*

Mary

1) The Mother of Jesus. According to tradition, she was the daughter of Joachim and Anne, of the lineage of David. While engaged to the carpenter Joseph, she received a visit from the angel Gabriel, who announced that she would become the mother of Jesus, the Messiah and Son of God. Mary consented. Mary rarely appears in the public life of Jesus. She was present at Jesus' first miracle at the wedding in Cana; and at the moment of the crucifixion, she was at the foot of the cross. The Church has given Mary the title "the mother of God," since Jesus is divine. The Church also teaches that Mary was conceived free from original sin, remained a virgin throughout her life and was taken up to heaven body and soul—because of her close association with Jesus, Son of God *(Matthew 1:16, 18-2:23; Mark 3:31-35; 6:3; Luke 1:26-2:52; 8:19-21; 11:27-28; John 2:1-12; 19:26; Acts 1:14; Galatians 4:4).*

2) The sister of Martha. She lived in Bethany, with her sister and her brother Lazarus. She loved to listen to Jesus. A few days before Jesus died, Mary anointed his feet with oil and dried them with her hair *(Luke 10:38-42; John 11:1-44; 12:1-8).*

3) Mary Magdalene, a disciple of Jesus who had been cured by him. She was the first known person to see the risen Jesus, and she ran to announce his resurrection to the apostles *(Mark 16:9-11; Luke 8:2; 24:10-11; John 20:1-18).*

4) Mary of Clopas. One of the women (together with Jesus' mother and Mary Magdalene) who was at Calvary when Jesus was crucified. This Mary may be the same person as the mother of

James and Joses, whom Matthew and Mark say was present on Calvary. If so, she was also one of the women who discovered the empty tomb of Jesus *(Matthew 27:56; 28:1-10; Mark 15:47; 16:1-8; John 19:25)*.

5) Mary, mother of the evangelist Mark. Her home was a gathering place for the Christians of Jerusalem *(Acts 12:12)*.

Matthew

Also called Levi, one of the twelve apostles. The first Gospel bears his name. He was a tax collector in Capernaum before Jesus said, "Follow me!" His missionary activity in the holy land and elsewhere is recorded in many ancient traditions but difficult to prove. His martyrdom is also controversial *(Matthew 9:9-13; 10:3; Luke 5:27-32)*.

Matthias

A disciple of Jesus who became one of the twelve apostles after the death of Judas Iscariot *(Acts 1:15-26)*.

Michael

The archangel mentioned in the *Book of Revelation*. He engaged in a battle against the forces of evil. The name "Michael" means "who is like God?" *(Revelation 12:7-9)*

Nathanael

(See Bartholomew.)

Nicodemus

An influential Pharisee, a doctor of the law and member of the Sanhedrin. He went at night to find Jesus and question him about the kingdom of God and about how to enter it. He had the courage to defend Jesus before the Sanhedrin. He and Joseph of Arimathea prepared Jesus' body for burial *(John 3:1-21; 7:50-52; 19:39-42)*.

Onesimus

A slave of Philemon, a Christian from Colossae and friend of Paul. The apostle met Onesimus after he had escaped from his master. The slave became a Christian and Paul wrote a letter to Philemon, asking him to pardon Onesimus and treat him as a brother *(Colossians 4:9; Philemon)*.

Onesiphorus

A Christian who helped Paul in Ephesus. Later he visited and comforted the apostle while he was in prison in Rome *(2 Timothy 1:16; 4:19)*.

Paul

The "apostle of the Gentiles" (pagans). He was born in Tarsus in Cilicia (Asia Minor) between

A.D. 5 and 10 and died a martyr in Rome under the Emperor Nero, probably in A.D. 64 or 67. Originally called by his Hebrew name, Saul, he was a persecutor of the early Christians. Then, on the way to Damascus, he was struck by a supernatural power: Jesus appeared to him ("Saul, Saul, why do you persecute me?"). From that moment on, he became a preacher of the new faith. He was a great traveler and a very hard worker, founder of church communities, an extraordinary preacher, and the author of several of our New Testament letters. He was imprisoned twice in Rome and eventually beheaded *(Acts 7:58; 8:1, 3; 9:1-30; 11:25-30; 12:25-28:31; the Pauline letters; 2 Peter 3:15-16).*

Peter

The leader of the apostles and of the primitive Church. His original name was Simon and he was a fisherman on the Sea of Galilee. Jesus stayed at his house in Capernaum. In the Gospels, the list of apostles begins with his name: "Simon also called Peter...." He died in Rome, crucified upside down sometime between A.D. 62 and 67. His bones were buried on Vatican Hill, where he died. Two New Testament letters bear his name *(Matthew 4:18-20, 10:2, 14:28-31, 16:13-23, 17:1-13, 24-27, 26:31-46, 69-75, Mark 1:16-18, 29-39, 5:37, 8:27-33, 9:2-8, 14:27-42, 66-72, 16:7, Luke—parallels, plus 22:8-13, 31-32, 24:34, John 1:40-42, 18:10-11, 15-27, 20:2-9, 21:1-22).*

Philemon

A Christian from Colossae, friend of Paul and master of the fugitive slave, Onesimus *(Philemon).*

Philip

1) One of the twelve apostles, who came from Bethsaida in Galilee, the city on the lake that was the hometown of Peter and Andrew. In the list of apostles he always has the fifth position, generally paired with Bartholomew. He is said to have evangelized Scythia and Phrygia. According to tradition he was crucified upside-down (like Peter) in a city in Asia Minor *(Matthew 10:3; John 1:43-49; 6:5-7; 12:21-22; 14:8-9; Acts 1:13).*
2) The second of the seven deacons ordained by the Apostles. He is also called an "evangelist" to distinguish him from the apostle. He evangelized in Samaria, where he converted and baptized Simon the Magician. In Caesarea, in 58, he hosted Paul on his return from his third apostolic journey. An old tradition says that he was the bishop of Tralle, the city where he died *(Acts 6:5; 8:4-13, 26-40; 21:8-9).*
3) A son of Herod the Great. He lived in Rome and married Herodias, who left him for his half-brother, Herod Antipas *(Mark 6:17).*
4) Philip, another son of Herod the Great. Governor of Iturea until 33, he married Salome, daughter of Herodias *(Luke 3:1).*

Phoebe

A Christian woman whom Paul knew. She worked in the Church in Cenchreae, one of the two ports of Corinth, in Achaia *(Romans 16:1).*

Pontius Pilate

The Roman governor of Judea from A.D. 26 to 36. He is most noted for his part in the trial of Jesus. Even though Pilate was convinced of Jesus' innocence, he was afraid to stand up to those who demanded Jesus' death. He had Jesus whipped and crucified *(Mt 27:1-21, 11-31, 58, 62-66; Mark 15:1-20, 42-45; Luke 3:1; 13:1; 23:1-25; John 18:28-19:22)*.

Priscilla

(See Aquila.)

Publius

The official who governed the island of Malta when Paul and his companions were shipwrecked there during their voyage to Rome *(Acts 28:1-10)*.

Rhoda

A servant in the house of John Mark's mother in Jerusalem. She responded to Peter from behind the door after the angel freed him from prison *(Acts 12:12)*.

Salome

1) One of the women who looked after the needs of Jesus and his disciples in Galilee. Many believe her to be the wife of Zebedee and the mother of James and John. She was present at the crucifixion and was part of the group who went to the tomb to embalm the body of Jesus with spices *(Matthew 27:56; Mark 15:40; 16:1)*.
2) (See Herodias.)

Sapphira

(See Ananias.)

Saul

(See Paul.)

Sergius Paulus

A Roman proconsul in Cyprus. When he saw Paul's deeds, " he believed, because he was greatly amazed at the teaching about the Lord" *(Acts 13:7-12)*.

Silas

An influential Christian of the church of Jerusalem. He, Paul and Barnabas were sent to Antioch to communicate the decision of a Church meeting in Jerusalem. He traveled with Paul on his second missionary journey *(Acts 15:22; 18:5; 2 Corinthians 1:19; 1 Thessalonians 1:1; 2 Thessalonians 1:1; 1 Peter 5:12)*.

Simeon

The elderly man to whom God revealed that he would not die before he saw the Messiah. Forty days after Jesus' birth, when Joseph and Mary brought Jesus to the temple, Simeon recognized Jesus as the Messiah, took him in his arms, and praised God *(Luke 2:25-35)*.

Simon

1) Called the Zealot or Canaanean, one of the twelve apostles. According to tradition, he preached in Egypt and Persia, where he was crucified *(Matthew 10:4; Acts 1:13)*.
2) A brother (cousin) of Jesus *(Matthew 13:55)*.
3) The (cured) leper who invited Jesus to his house in Bethany *(Matthew 26:6; Mark 14:3)*.
4) The Pharisee with whom Jesus was dining when a woman known in the city as a "sinner" came to his house and bathed Jesus' feet with her tears of repentance *(Luke 7:36-50)*.
5) Simon of Cyrene, who was forced to carry the cross of Jesus *(Matthew 27:32)*.
6) A tanner of leather at Joppa, with whom Peter stayed on one of his missionary journeys *(Acts 9:43)*.

Simon the Magician

A Samaritan famous for his magic. He wanted to buy from Peter the power to communicate the gifts of the Spirit; this is where the term *simony* comes from *(Acts 9-24)*.

Sosthenes

1) Head of the synagogue at Corinth after Crispus converted to Christianity *(Acts 18:17)*.
2) A Christian known to the members of the Church at Corinth *(1 Corinthians 1:1)*.

Stephanas

The first Greek to become a Christian in Achaia (southern Greece) *(1 Corinthians 1:16; 16:15)*.

Stephen

The "protomartyr," that is, the first martyr of the Christian faith. He was one of the seven deacons chosen by the Christian community of Jerusalem. Accused of having blasphemed against God and against the law of Moses, he was stoned to death. Among the crowd that was stoning him was Saul, the future Paul, not yet converted *(Acts 6:1-7:60)*.

Theophilus

The person to whom Luke dedicated his Gospel and the *Acts of the Apostles*. The name means "friend of God" *(Luke 1:3; Acts 1:1)*.

Theudas

Head of a band of four hundred rebels. When he was killed, his followers dispersed and the movement disbanded. Gamaliel recalled this episode at the trial of the apostles and said that the movement begun by Jesus would die out in the same way if it did not come from God *(Acts 5:34).*

Thomas

Also called the "Twin." He is one of the twelve apostles, commonly known for his disbelief when Jesus appeared after his resurrection. According to tradition, he carried out his apostolate in India, where he died a martyr *(John 11:16; 14:5; 20:24-29; 21:1; Acts 1:12).*

Tiberias

The emperor of Rome at the time of Jesus (A.D. 12-37). In the Gospels he is called by the title "Caesar" *(Luke 3:1).*

Timothy

A native of Lystra in Lycaonia, Asia Minor. He was the son of a pagan father and a Hebrew mother who had converted to Christianity. He became a disciple of Paul and followed him to Macedonia and Achaia. Then he went to Rome and later to Ephesus, where, according to tradition, he was made bishop and later suffered martyrdom *(Acts 16:1-3; 17:14-15; 1 Corinthians 4:17; 1 Thessalonians 1:1; 3:1; 1 and 2 Timothy).*

Titus

A Christian of Gentile origin and a follower of Paul. He is thought to have governed the Church in Crete *(1 Corinthians 16:10; 2 Corinthians 2:13; 7:13; 8; 12:18; Galatians 2; 2 Timothy 4:10; Titus).*

Trophimus

A Christian of Ephesus, who accompanied Paul on part of his third journey *(Acts 20:4; 21:29; 2 Timothy 4:20).*

Tychicus

One of Paul's friends and collaborators. He was close to Paul in many circumstances, including Paul's last imprisonment in Rome. As Paul reached the end of his life, he sent his friend to Ephesus to help the Christians of that city *(Acts 20:4; Ephesians 6:21; Colossians 4:7; 2 Timothy 4:12; Titus 3:12).*

Zacchaeus

The head of the tax collectors in Jericho. He welcomed Jesus into his home and gave half of his goods to the poor *(Luke 19:1-10).*

Zebedee

A fisherman, the father of the apostles James and John *(Matthew 4:21).*

Zechariah

A priest, the husband of Elizabeth and father of John the Baptist. When an angel announced that he would have a son, he didn't believe and became mute until the birth of John *(Luke 1:5-25, 59-79)*.

St. Paul Book & Media Centers

ALASKA
750 West 5th Ave., Anchorage, AK 99501   907-272-8183

CALIFORNIA
3908 Sepulveda Blvd., Culver City, CA 90230   310-397-8676
5945 Balboa Ave., San Diego, CA 92111   619-565-9181
46 Geary Street, San Francisco, CA 94108   415-781-5180

FLORIDA
145 S.W. 107th Ave., Miami, FL 33174   305-559-6715

HAWAII
1143 Bishop Street, Honolulu, HI 96813   808-521-2731

ILLINOIS
172 North Michigan Ave., Chicago, IL 60601   312-346-4228

LOUISIANA
4403 Veterans Memorial Blvd., Metairie, LA 70006   504-887-7631

MASSACHUSETTS
50 St. Paul's Ave., Jamaica Plain, Boston, MA 02130
 617-522-8911
Rte. 1, 885 Providence Hwy., Dedham, MA 02026   617-326-5385

MISSOURI
9804 Watson Rd., St. Louis, MO 63126   314-965-3512

NEW JERSEY
561 U.S. Route 1, Wick Plaza, Edison, NJ 08817   908-572-1200

NEW YORK
150 East 52nd Street, New York, NY 10022   212-754-1110
78 Fort Place, Staten Island, NY 10301   718-447-5071

OHIO
2105 Ontario Street (at Prospect Ave.), Cleveland, OH 44115
 610-621-9427

PENNSYLVANIA
510 Holstein Street, Bridgeport, PA 19405; 215-277-7728

SOUTH CAROLINA
243 King Street, Charleston, SC 29401   803-577-0175

TENNESSEE
4811 Poplar Ave., Memphis, TN 38117   901-761-2987

TEXAS
114 Main Plaza, San Antonio, TX 78205   210-224-8101

VIRGINIA
1025 King Street, Alexandria, VA 22314   703-549-3806

GUAM
285 Farenholt Avenue, Suite 308, Tamuning, Guam 96911
 671-646-7745

CANADA
3022 Dufferin Street, Toronto, Ontario, Canada M6B 3T5
 416-781-9131